JULY 50 COLORING PAGES FOR OLDER KIDS RELAXATION

SHIH CHIEN HUA

PUBLISHED BY:
SHIH CHIEN HUA
Copyright © 2018

SEABIRD SHOP >50FOR

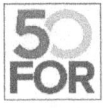

FB FAN PAGE

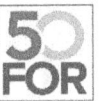

Disclaimer
The information contained in this book is for general information purposes only. The information is provided by the authors and while we endeavor to keep the information up to date and correct, we make no representations or warranties of any kind, express or implied, about the completeness, accuracy, reliability, suitability or availability with respect to the book or the information, products, services, or related graphics contained in the book for any purpose. Any reliance you place on such information is therefore strictly at your own risk.

JULY 1ST

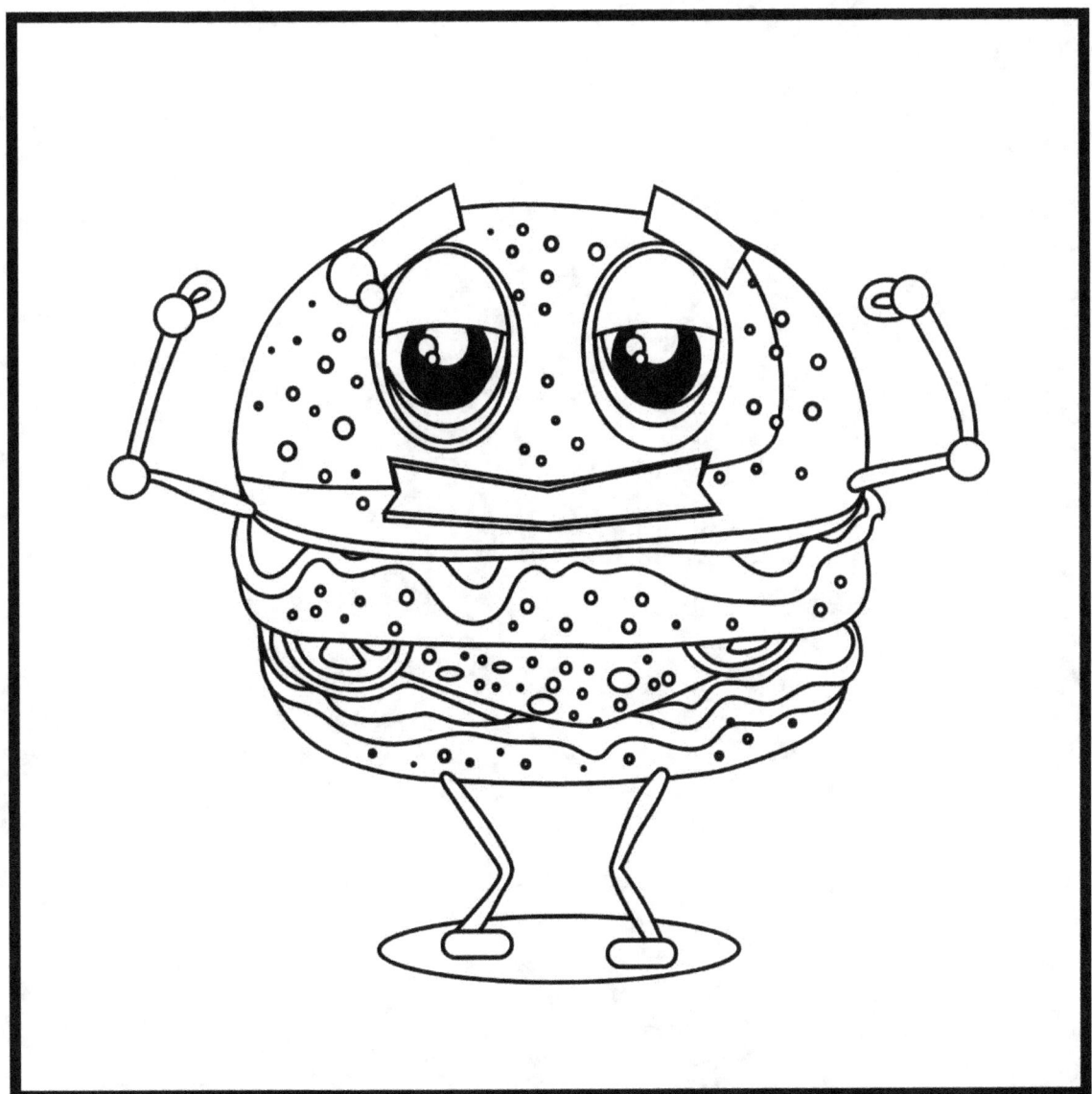

note:

_____

_____

_____

JULY 2ND

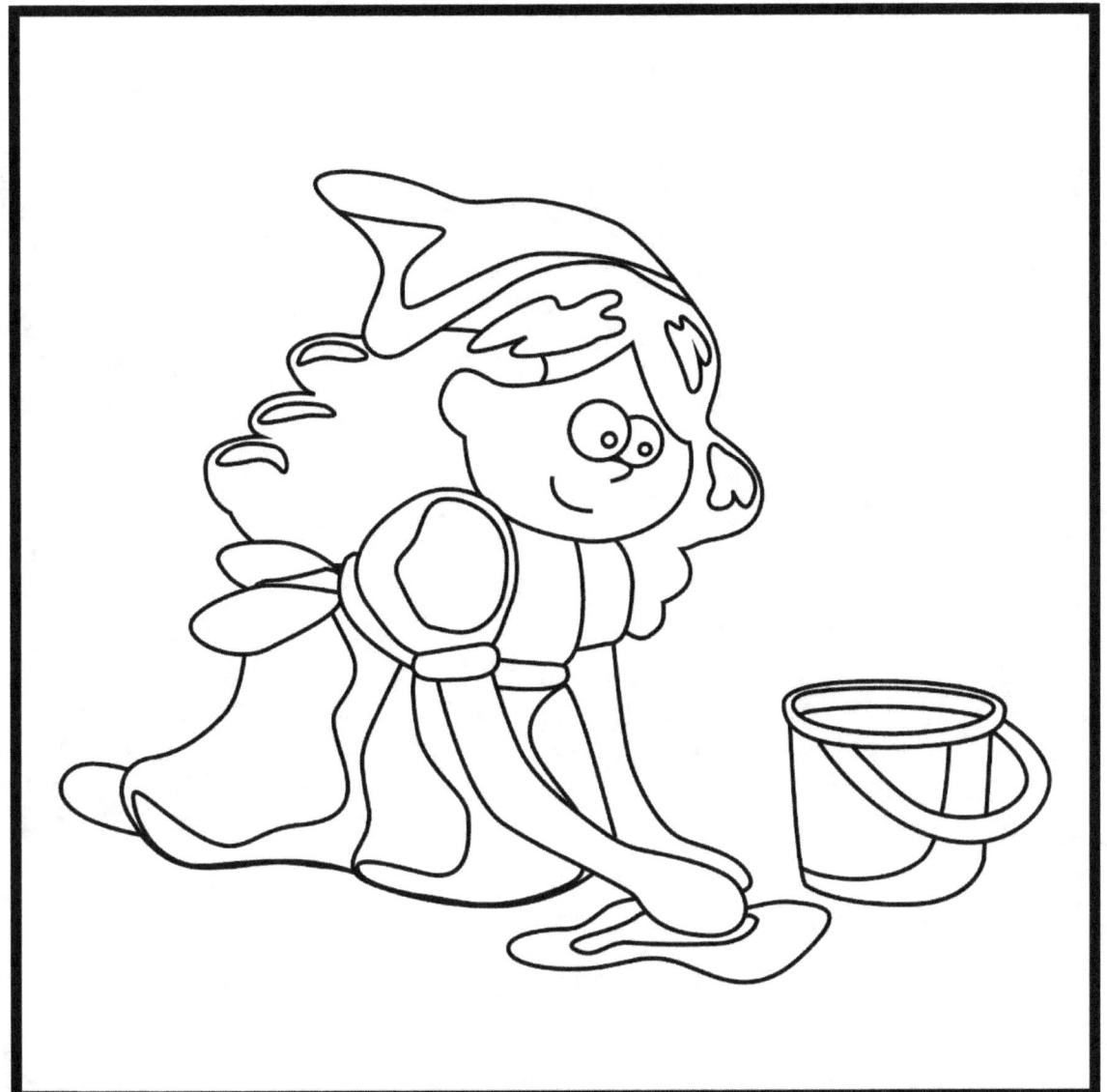

note:

_____

_____

_____

JULY 3rD

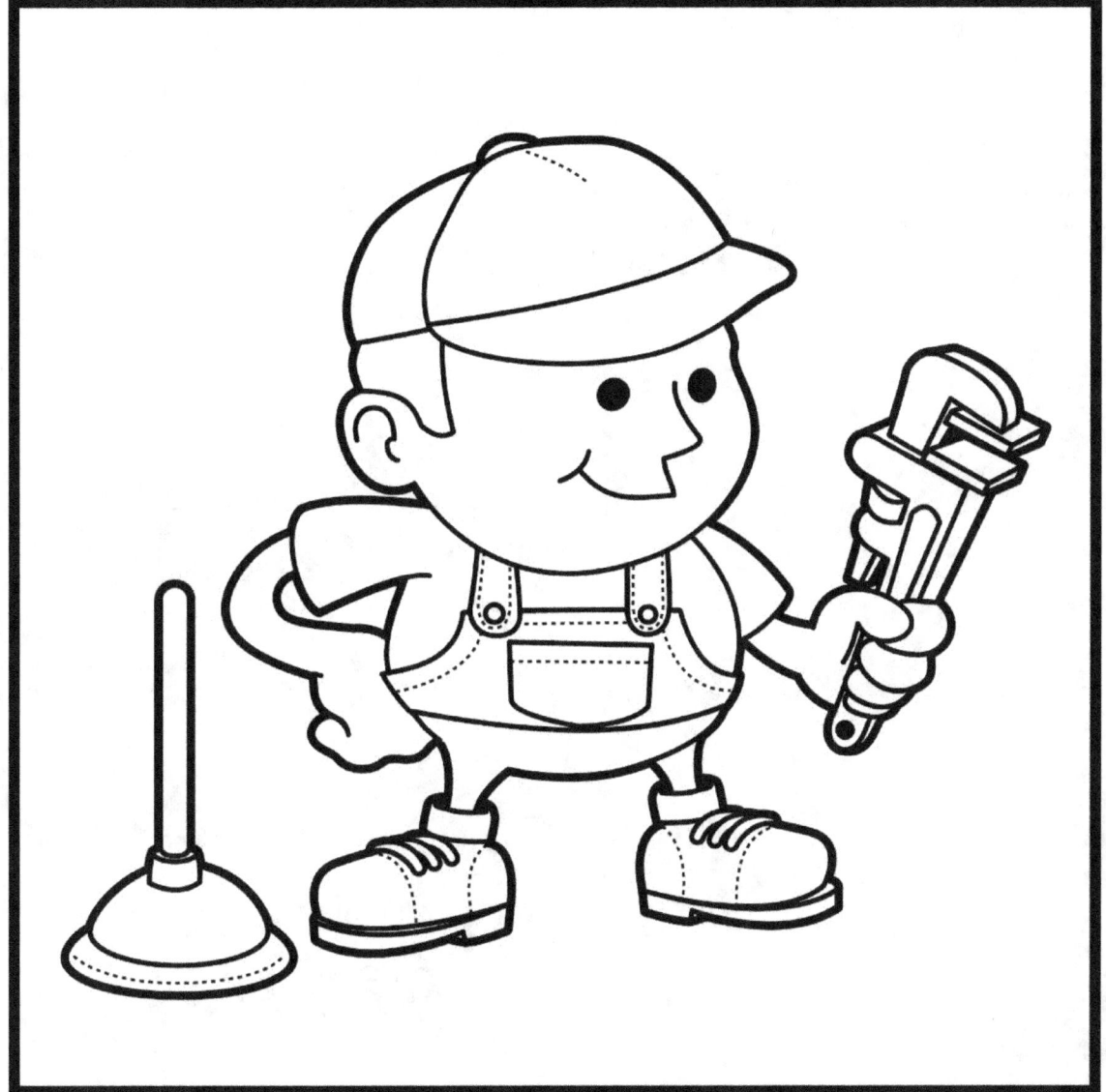

note:

_____

_____

_____

JULY 4TH

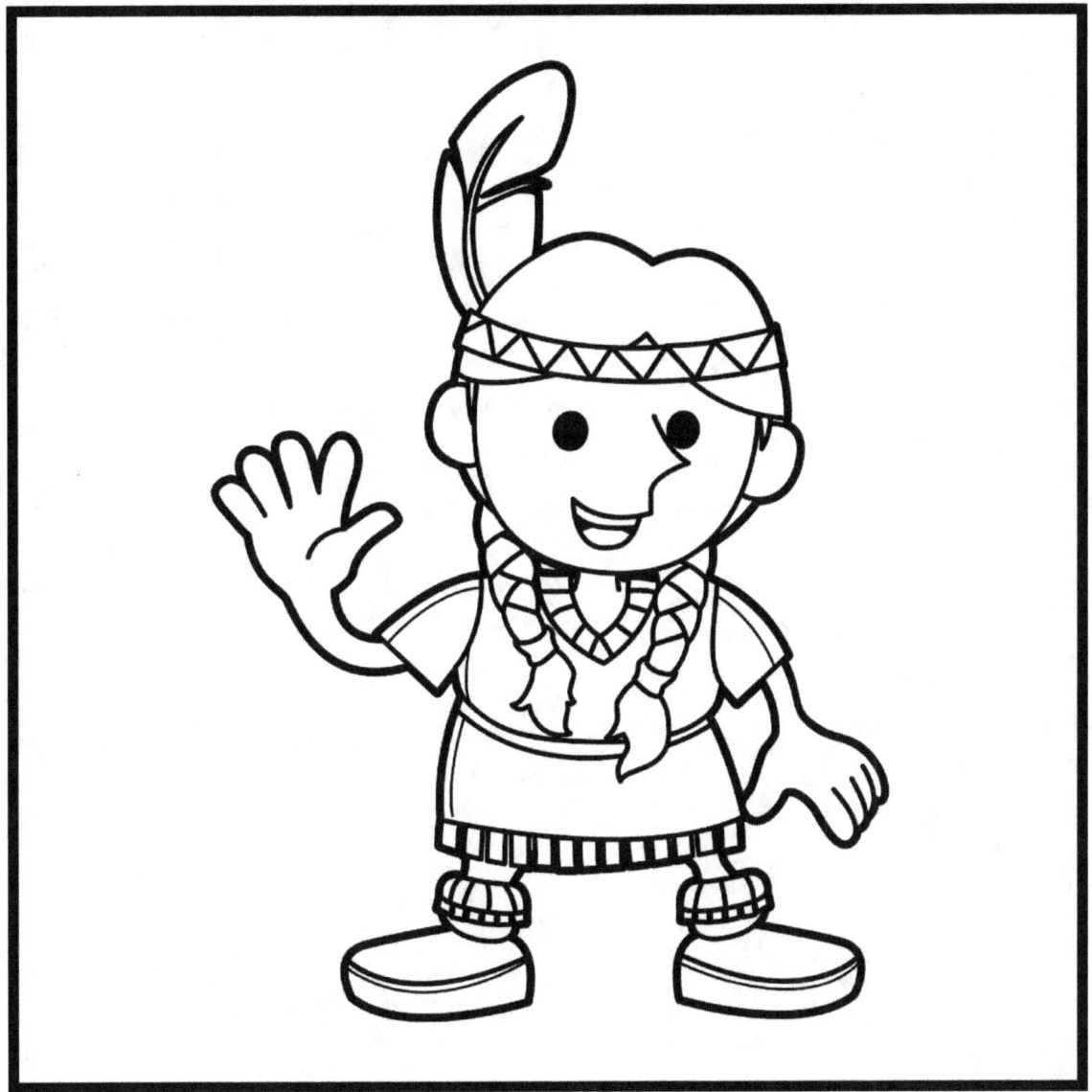

note:

_____

_____

_____

JULY 5TH

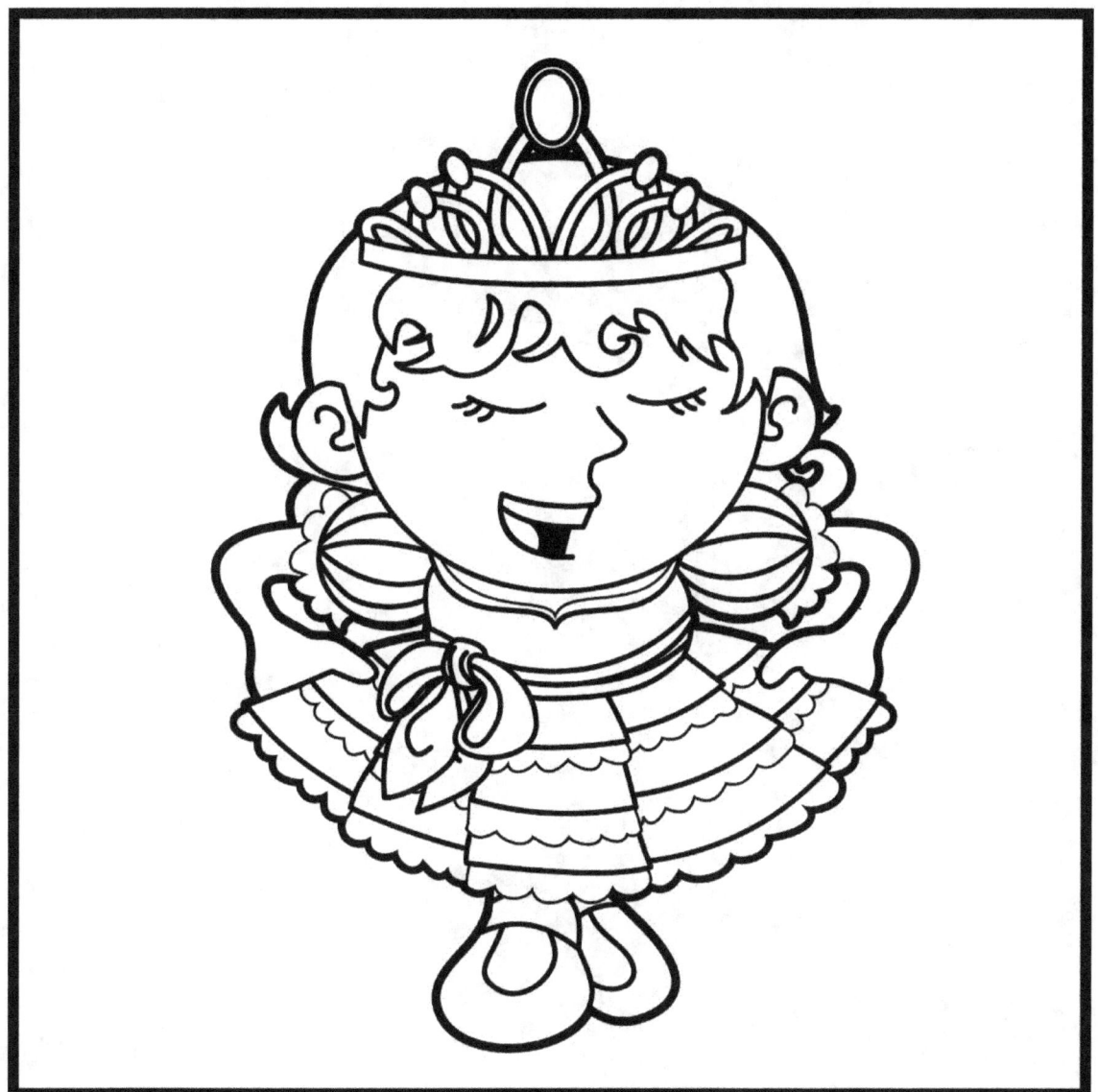

note:

_____

_____

_____

JULY 6TH

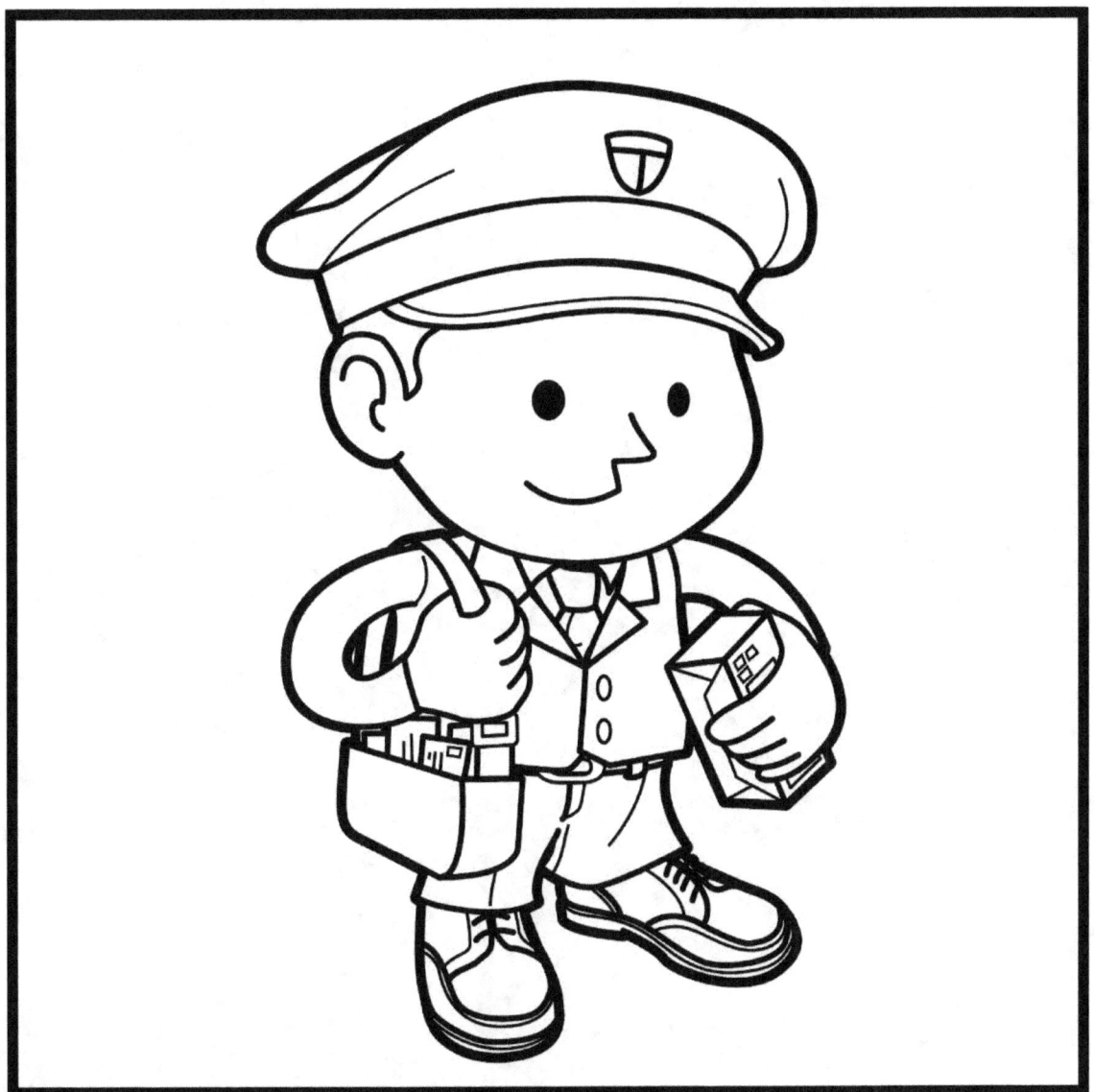

note:

_____

_____

_____

JULY 7TH

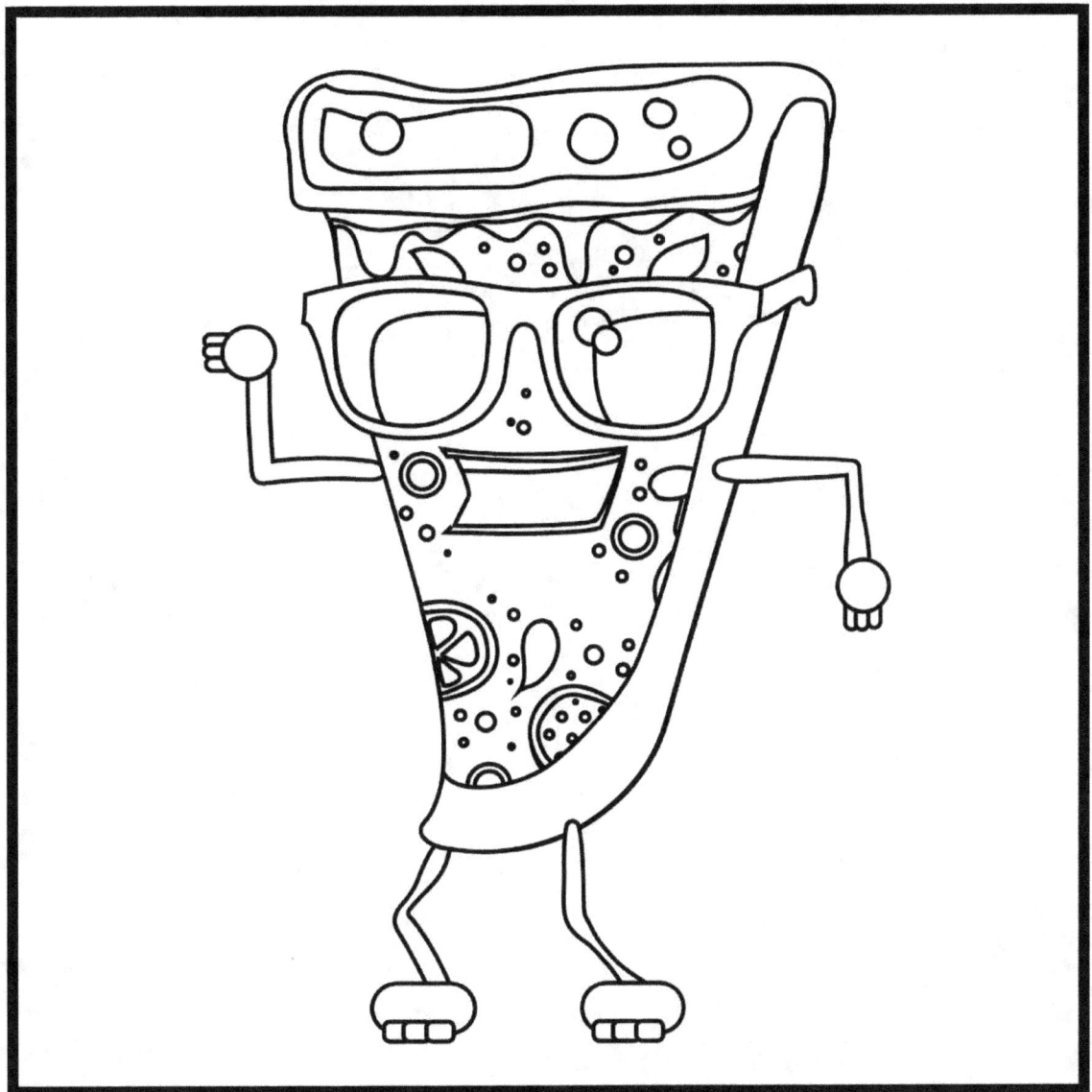

note:

_____

_____

_____

JULY 8TH

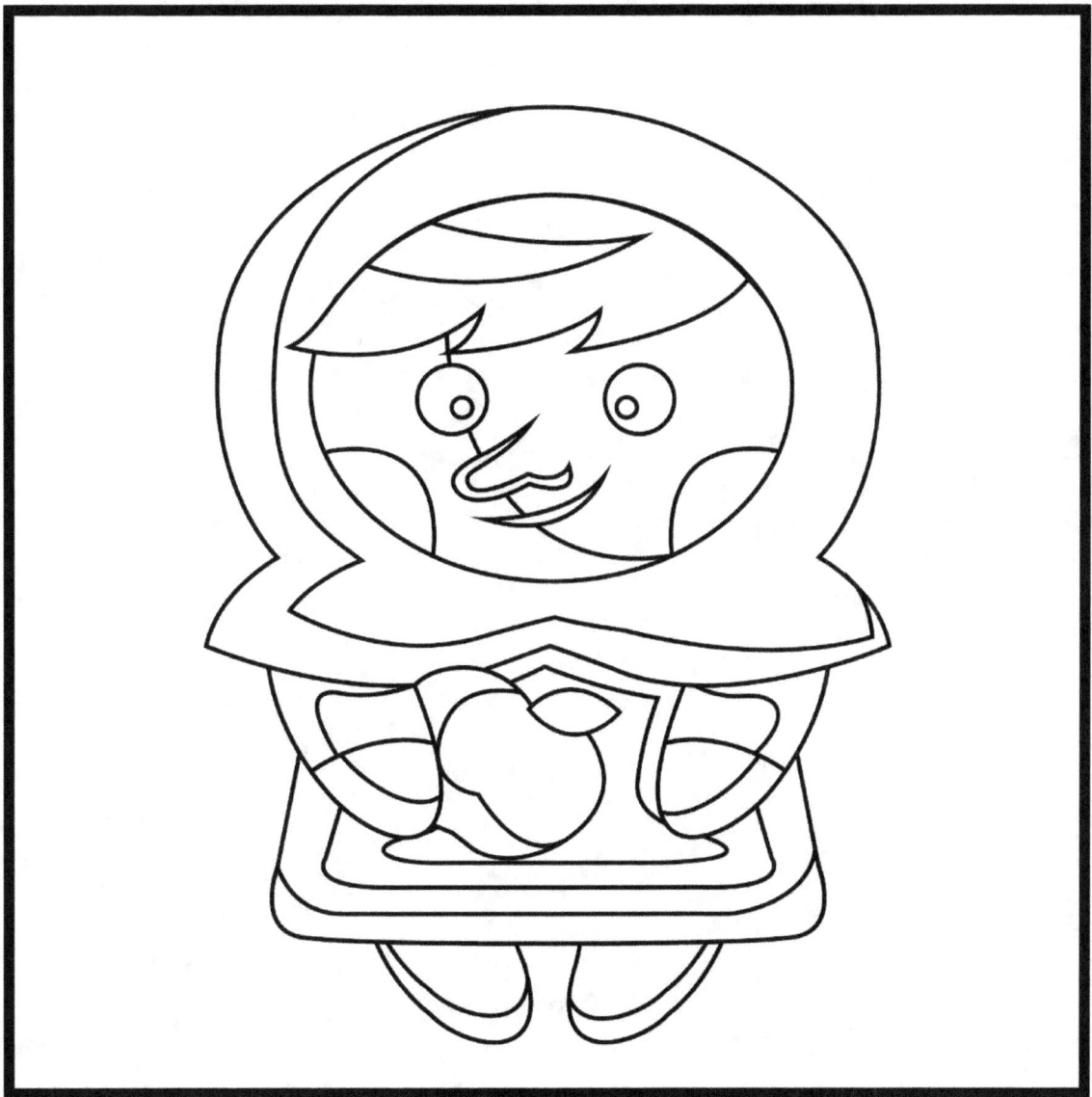

note:

_____

_____

_____

JULY 9TH

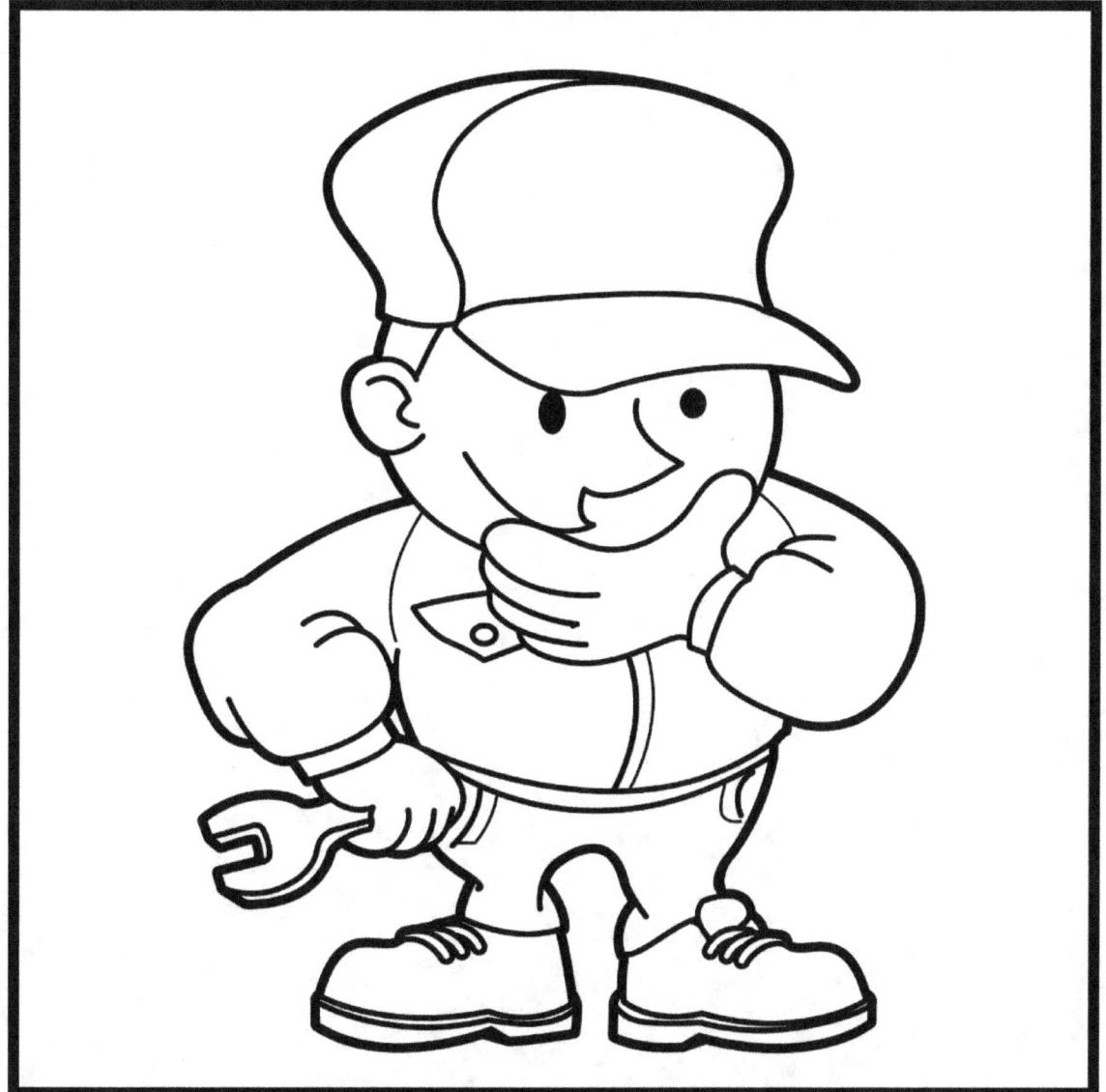

note:

_____

_____

_____

JULY 10TH

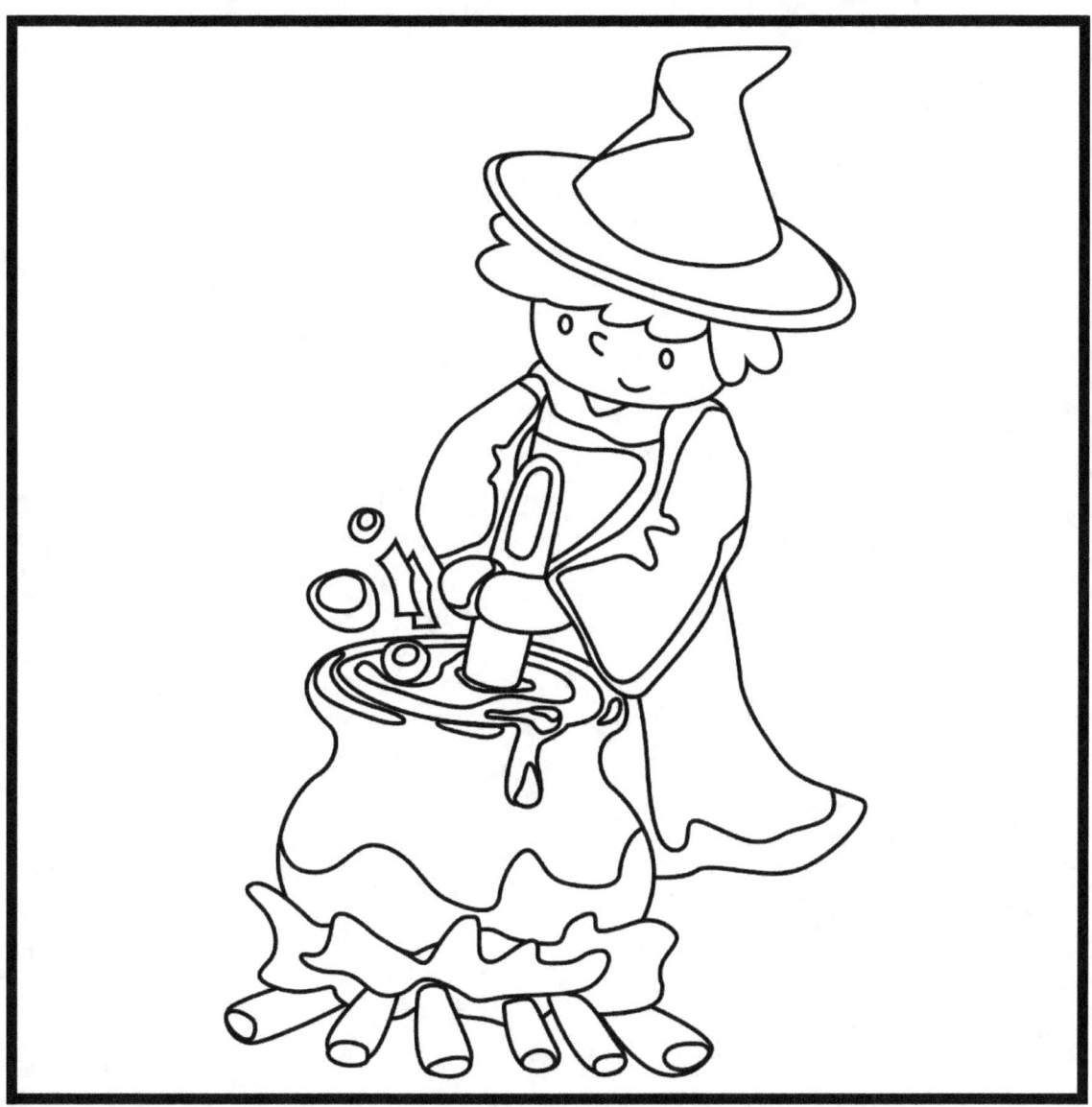

note:

_____

_____

_____

JULY 11TH

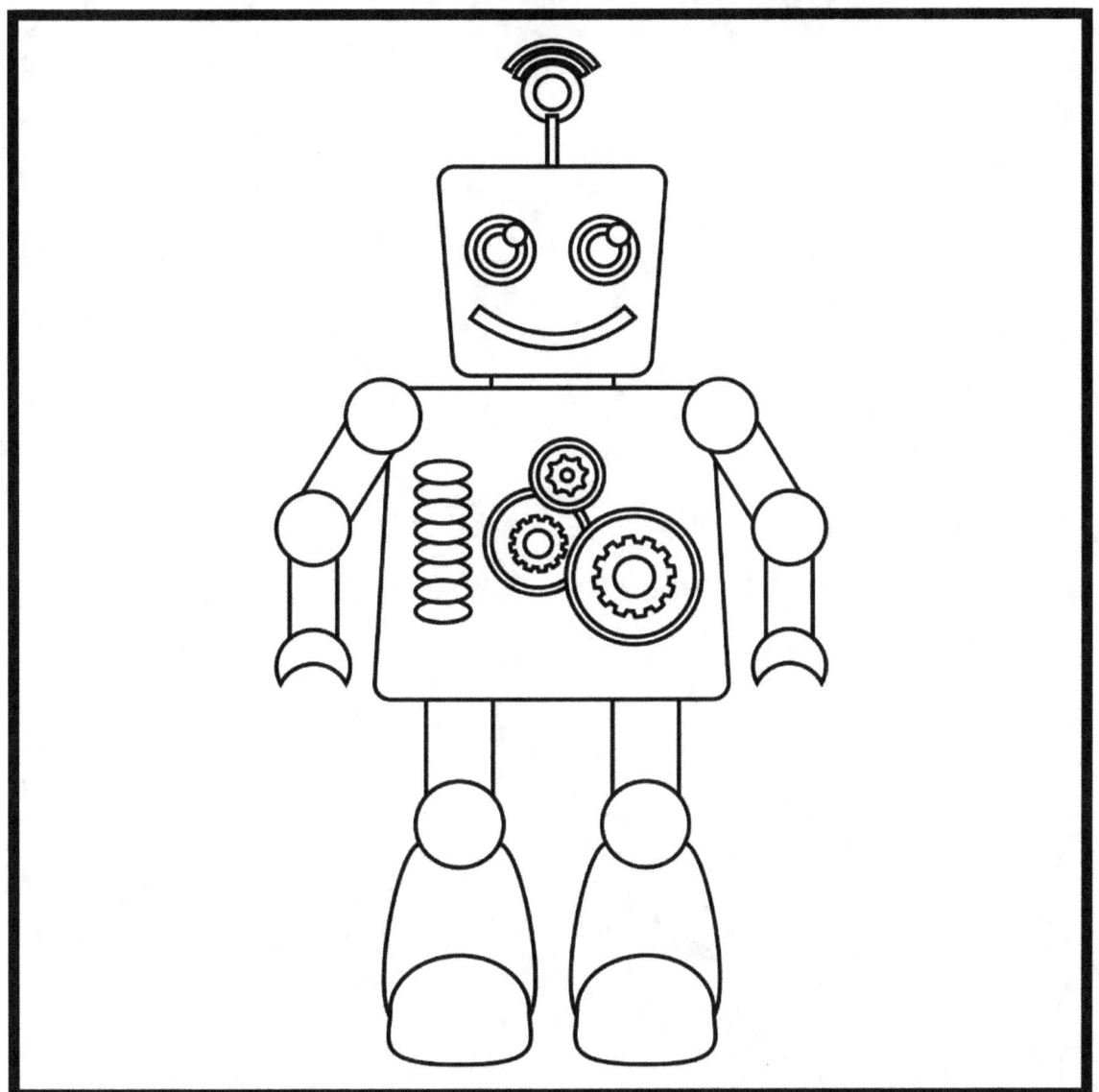

note:

_____

_____

_____

JULY 12TH

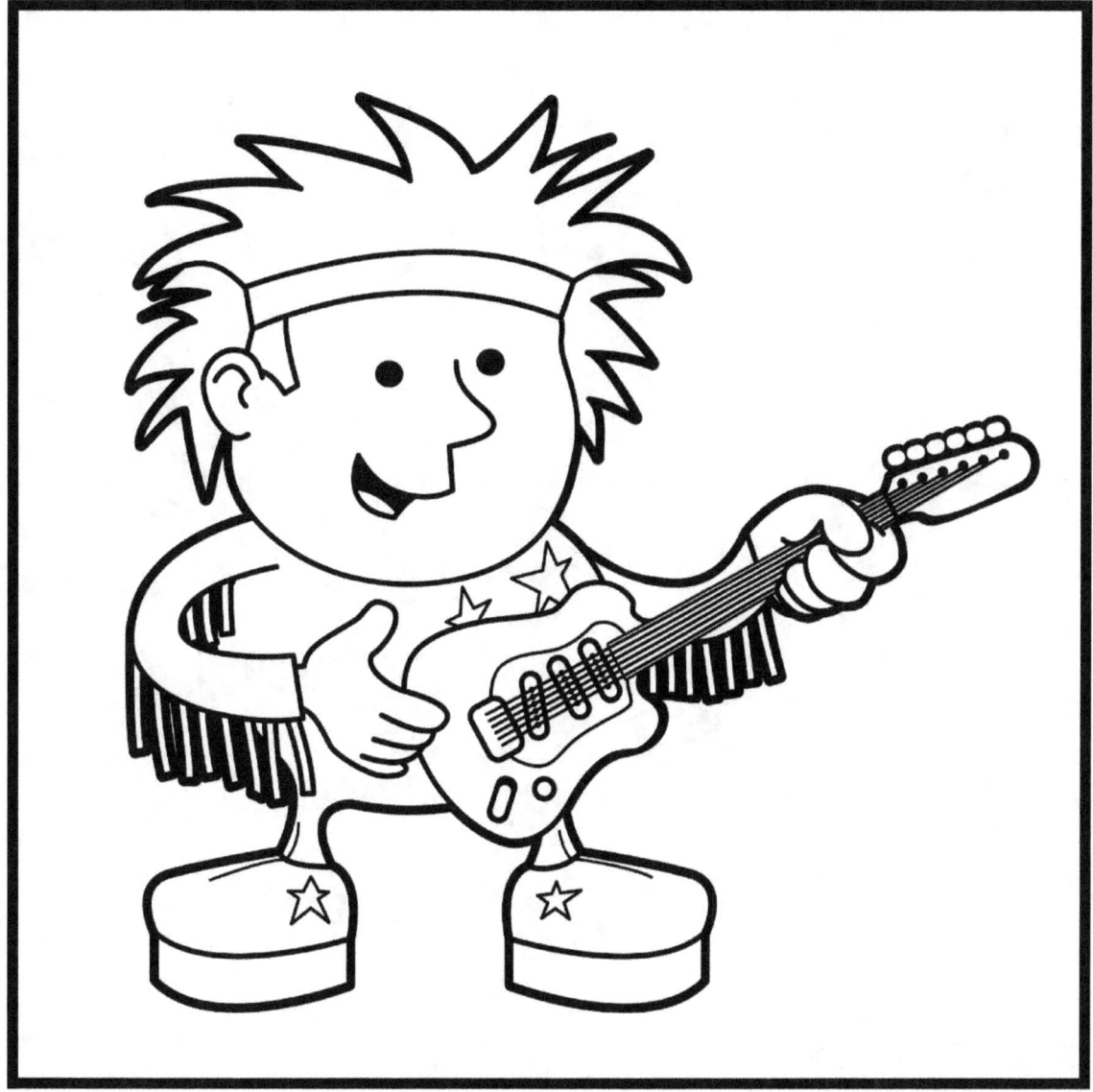

note:

_____

_____

_____

JULY 13TH

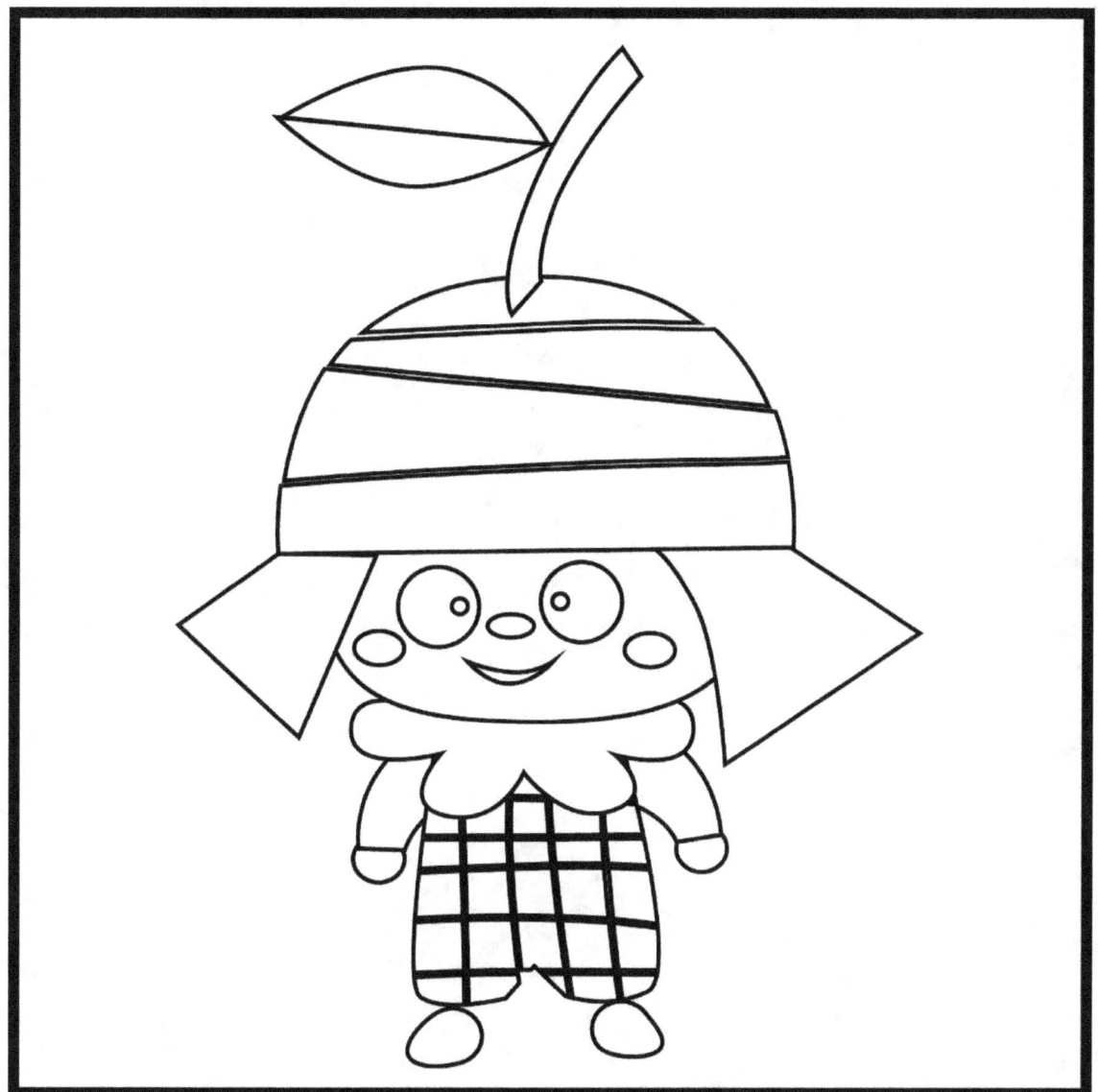

note:

_____

_____

_____

JULY 14TH

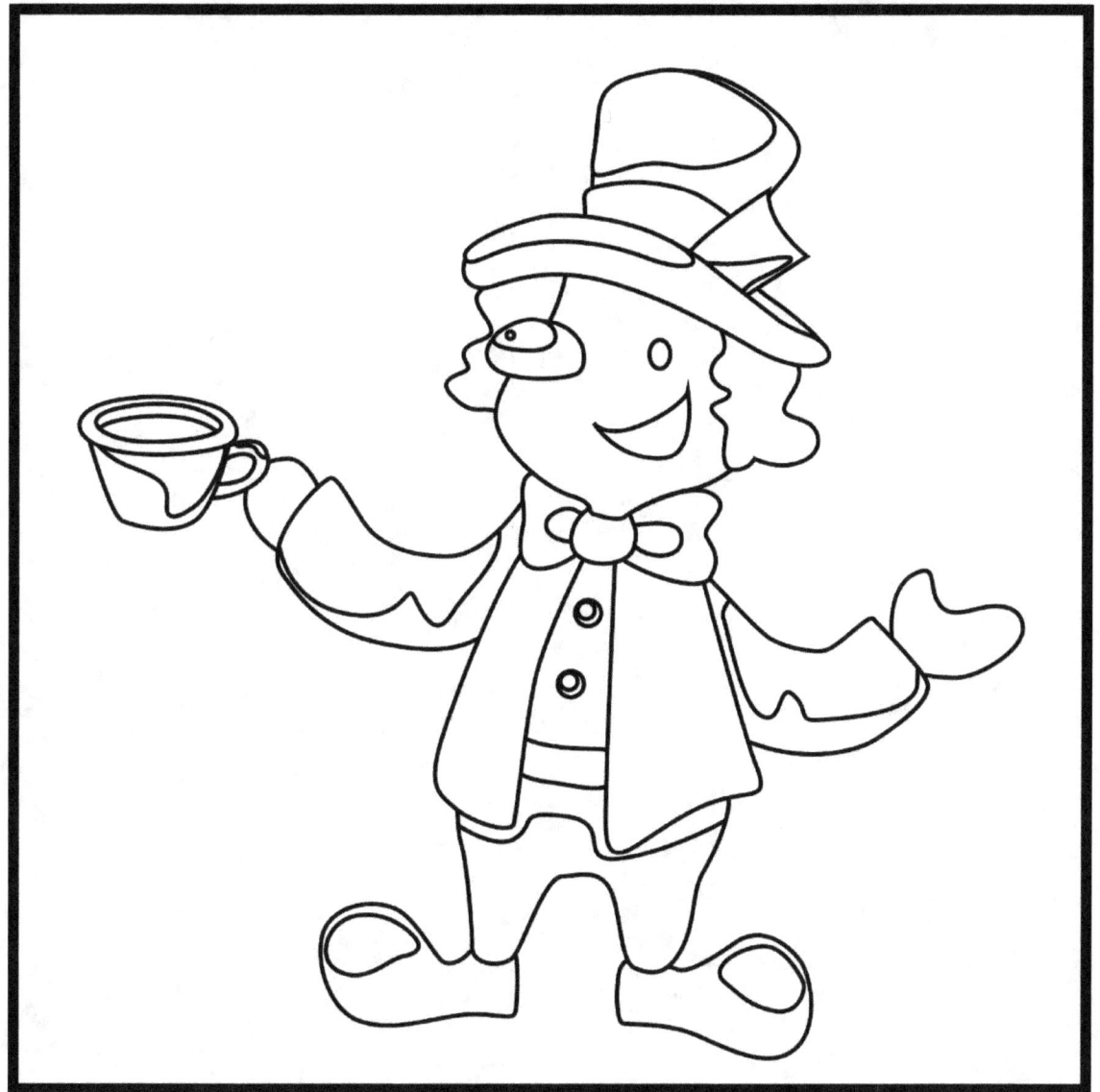

note:

_____

_____

_____

JULY 15TH

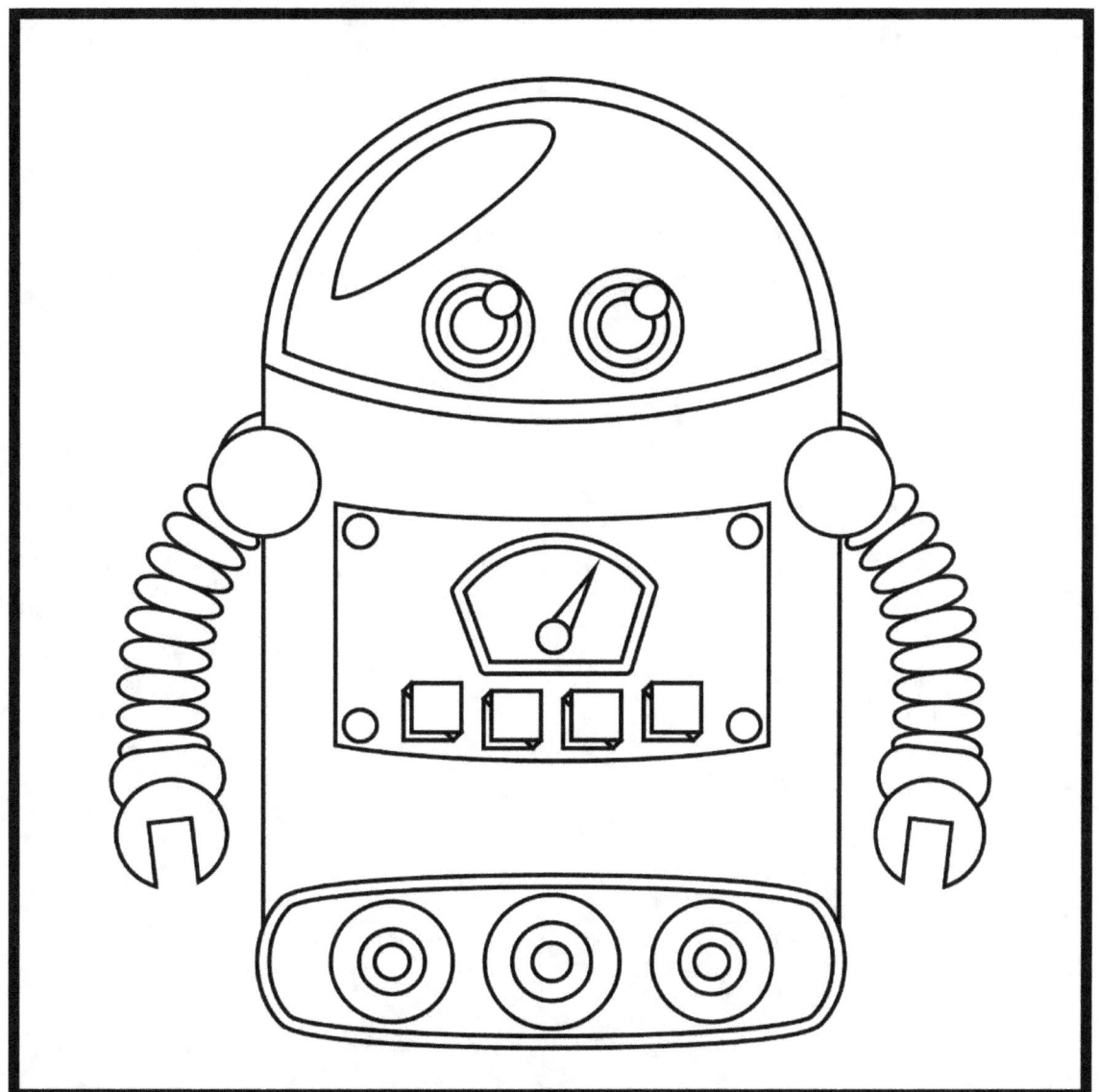

note:

_____

_____

_____

JULY 16TH

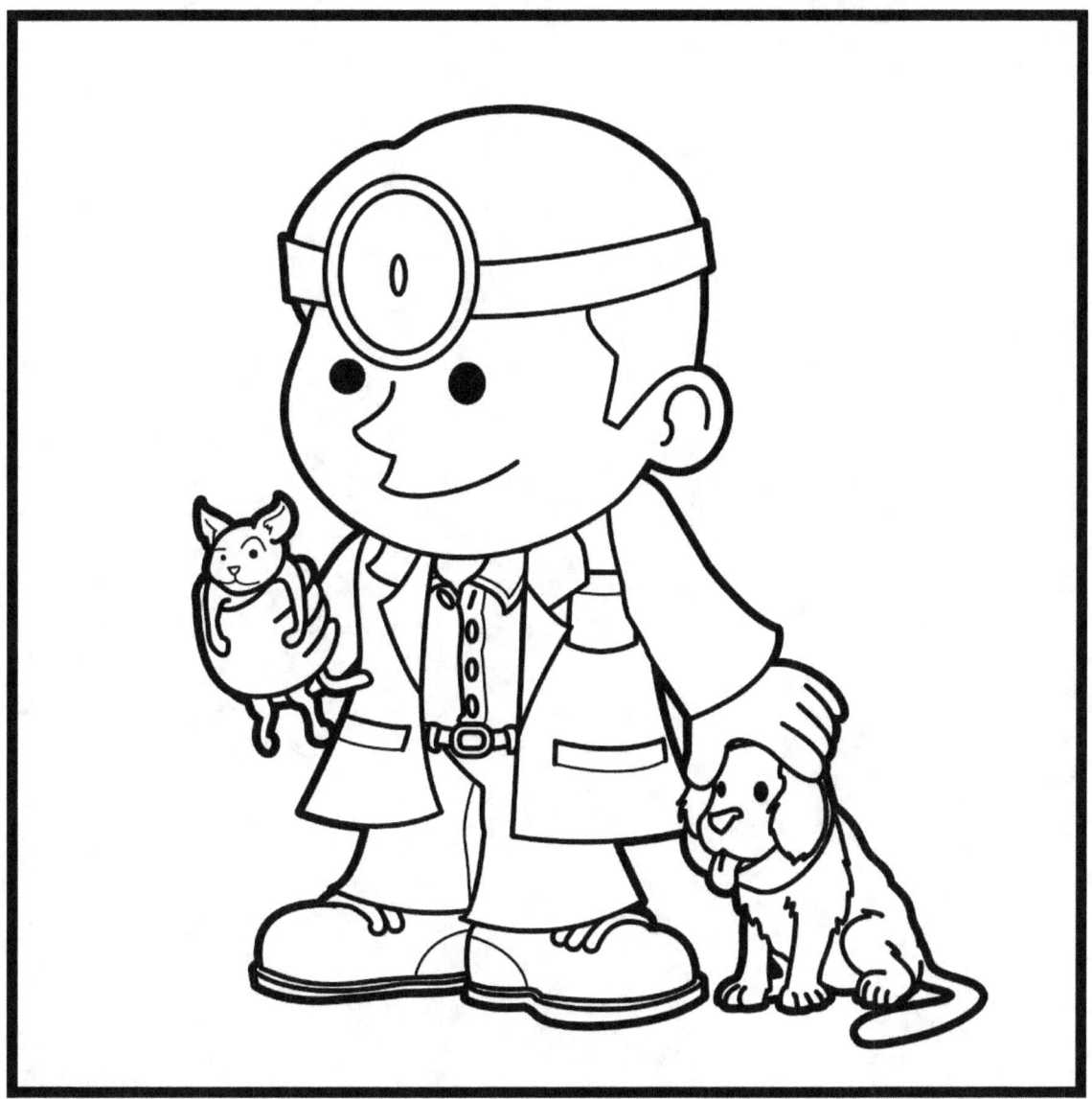

note:

_____

_____

_____

JULY 17TH

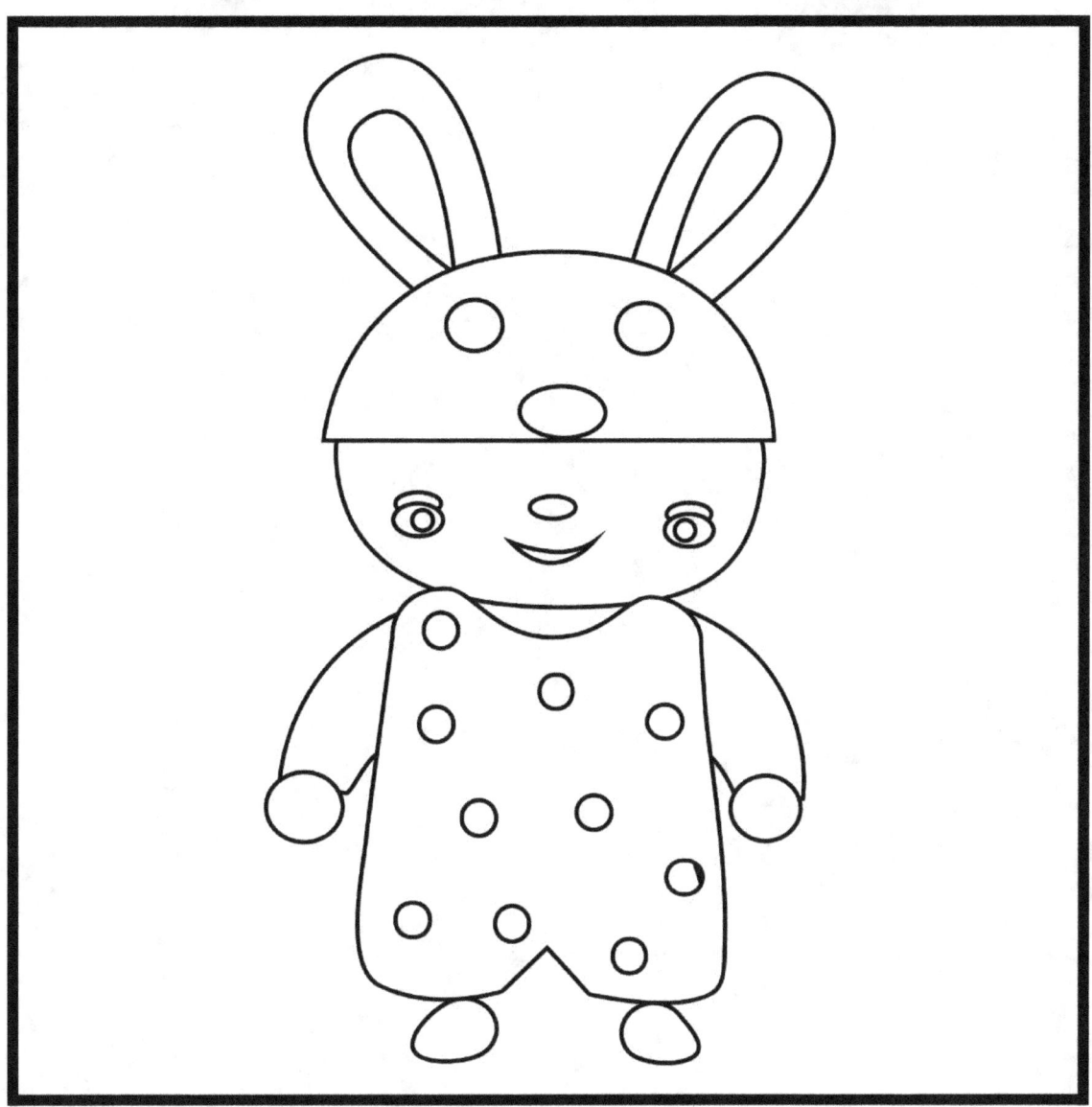

note:

_____

_____

_____

JULY 18TH

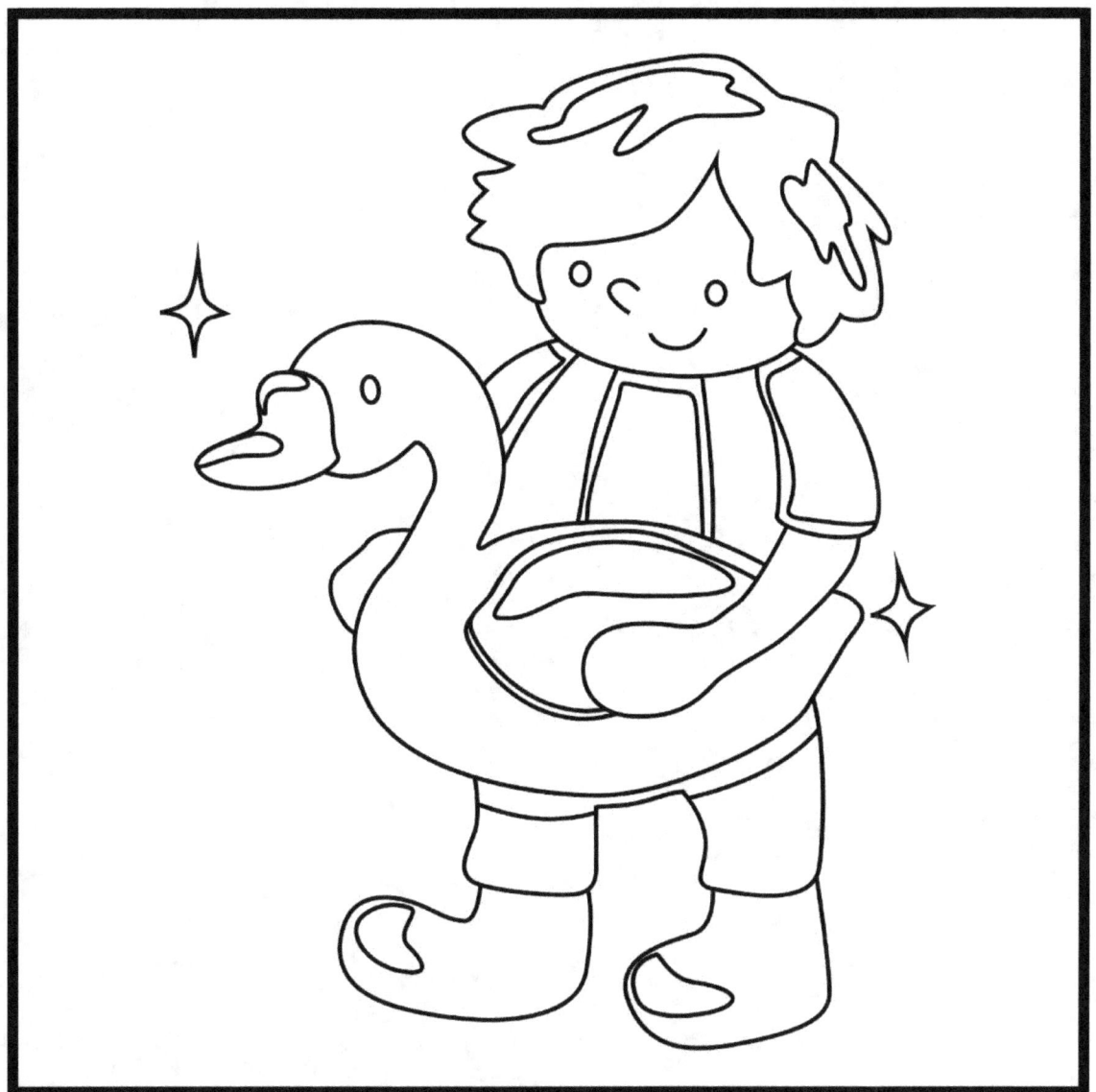

note:

_____

_____

_____

JULY 19TH

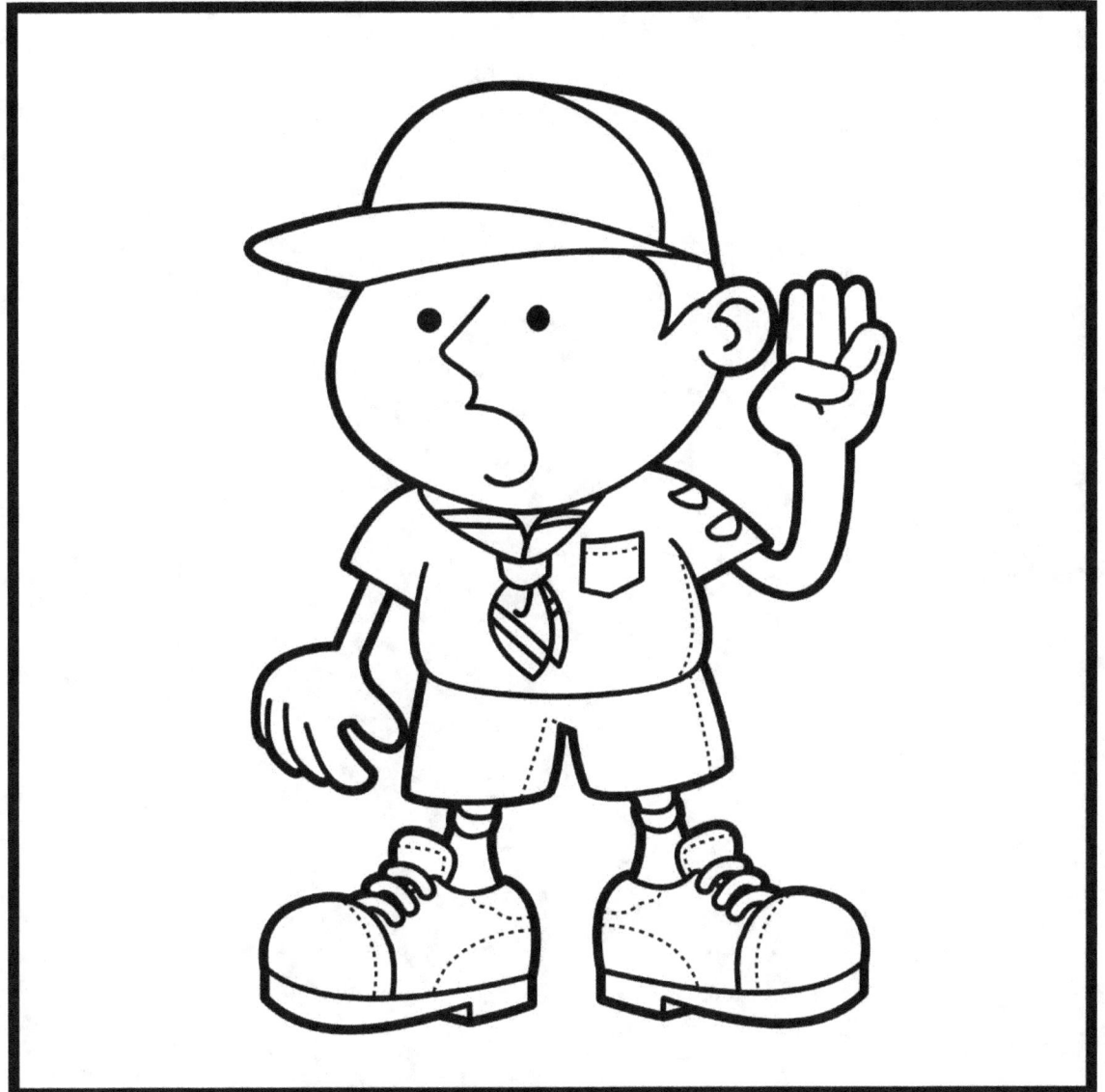

note:

_____

_____

_____

JULY 20TH

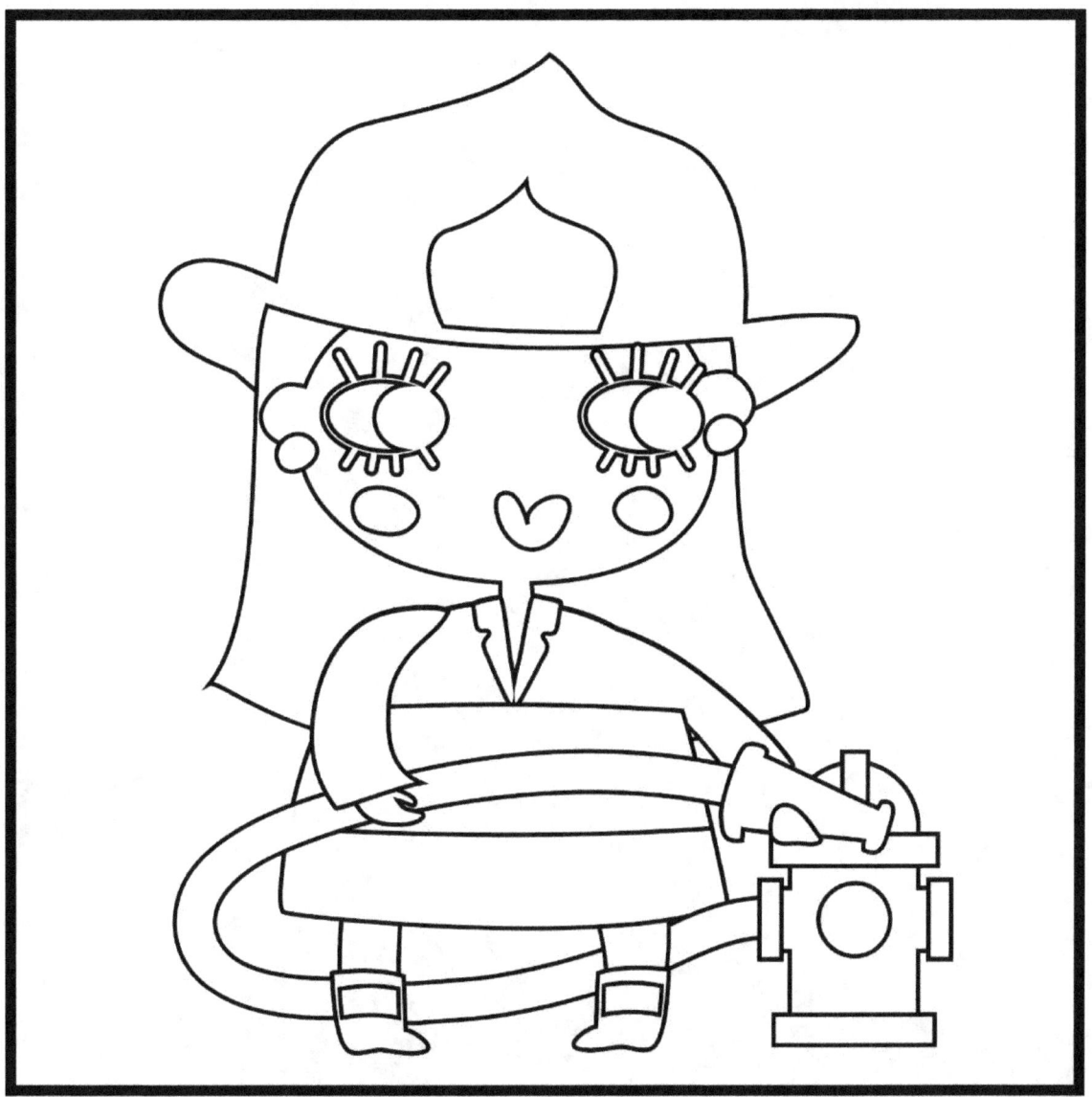

note:

_____

_____

_____

JULY 21TH

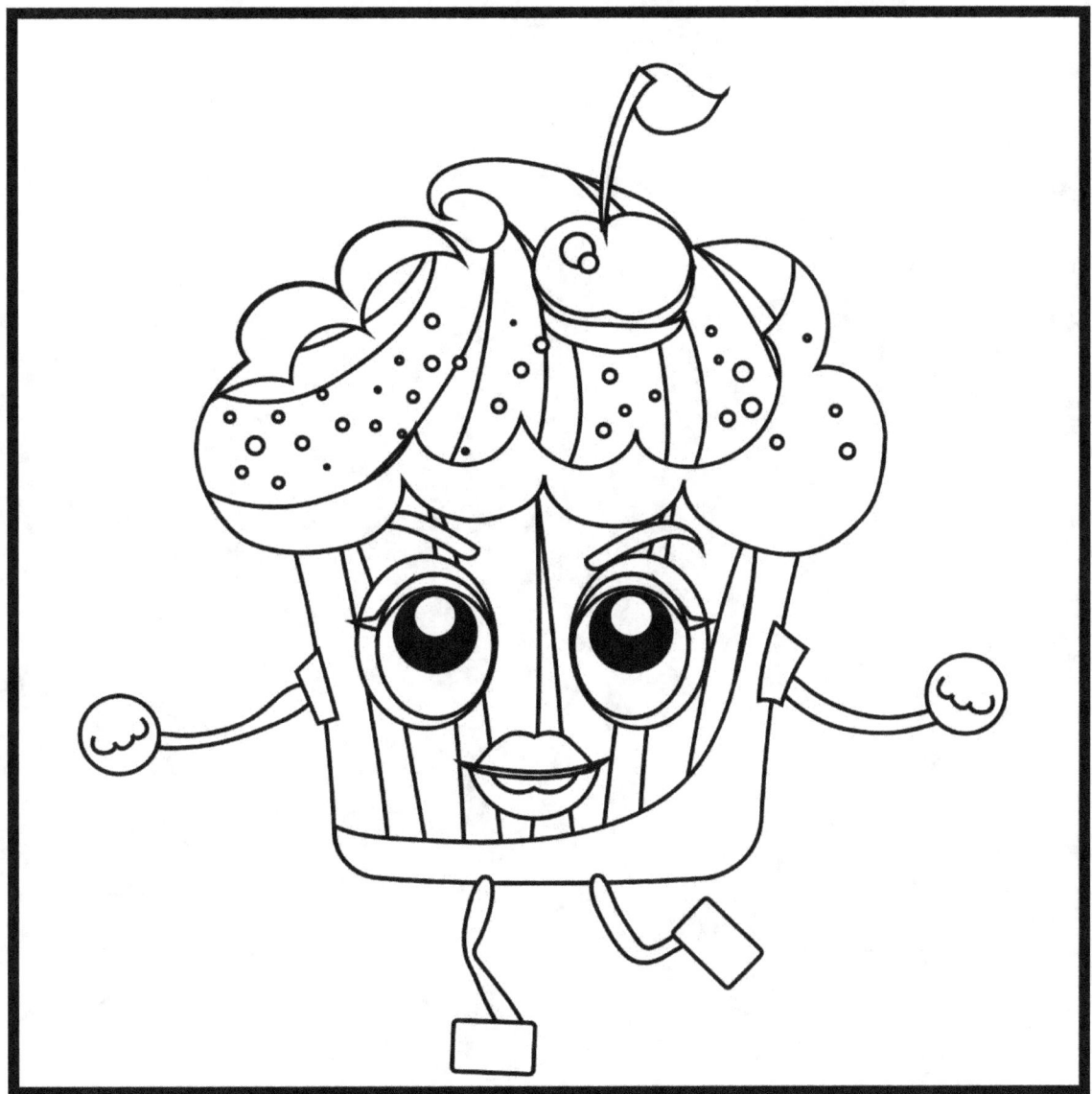

note:

_____

_____

_____

JULY 22TH

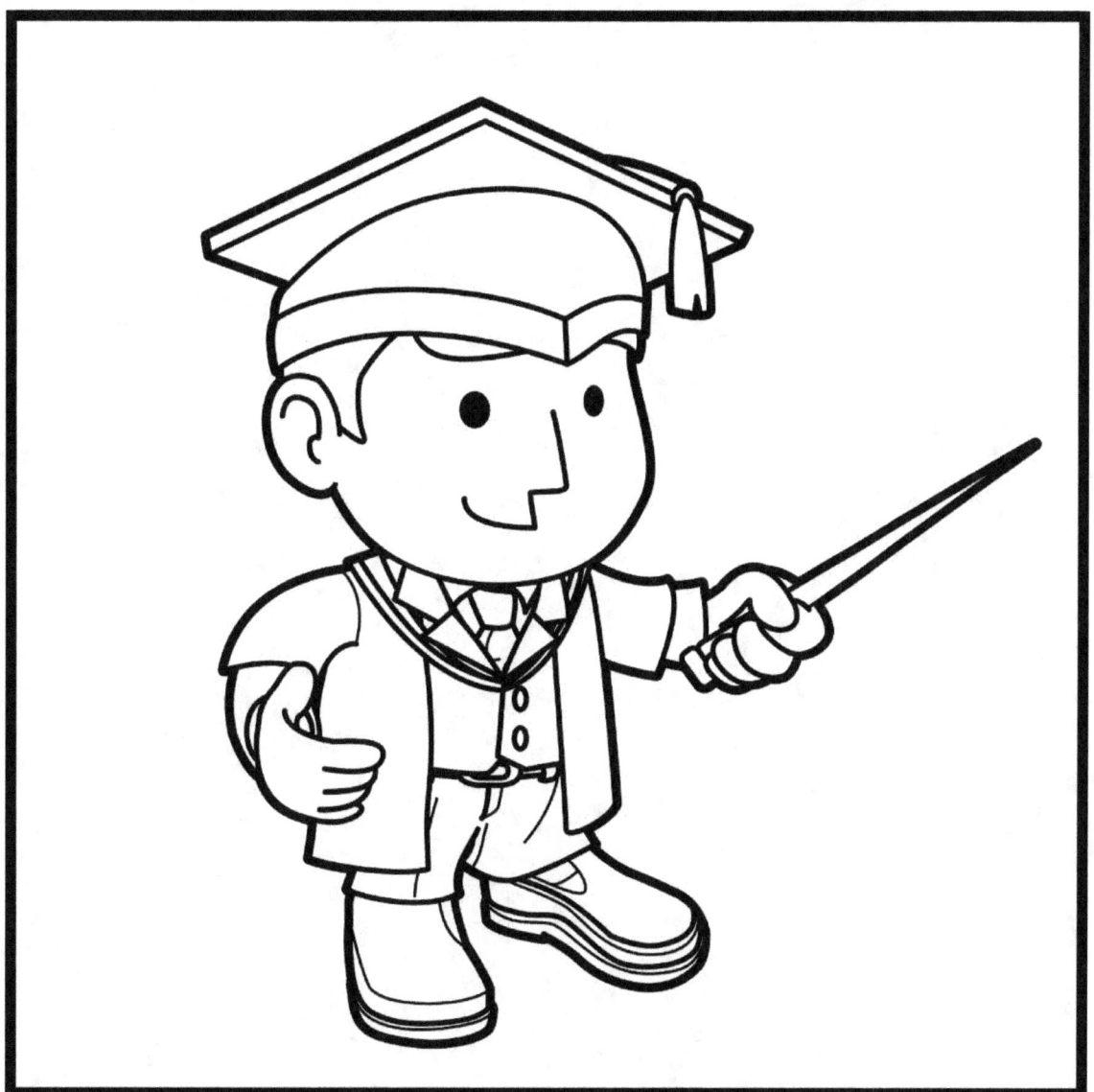

note:

_____

_____

_____

JULY 23TH

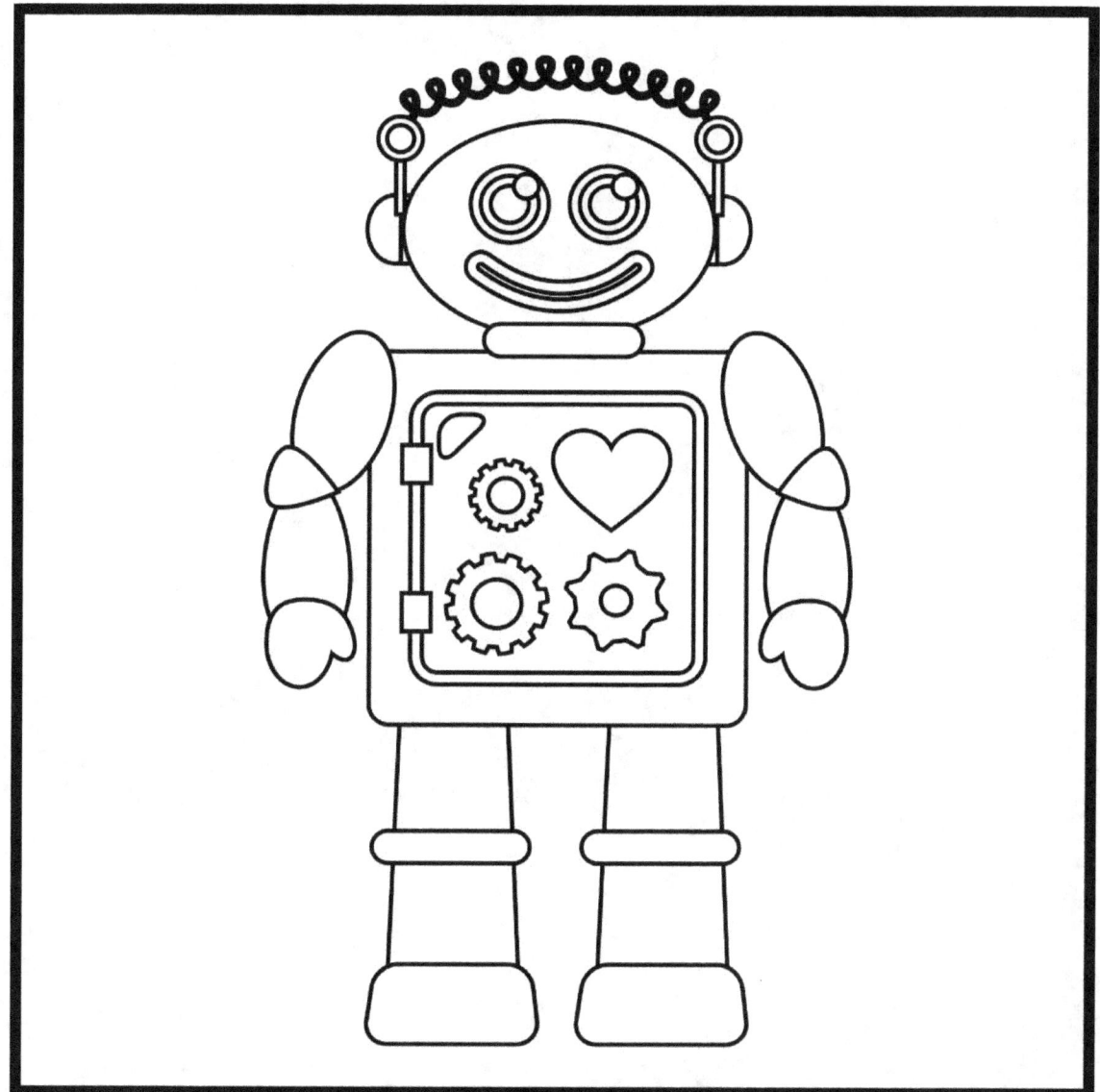

note:

_____

_____

_____

JULY 24TH

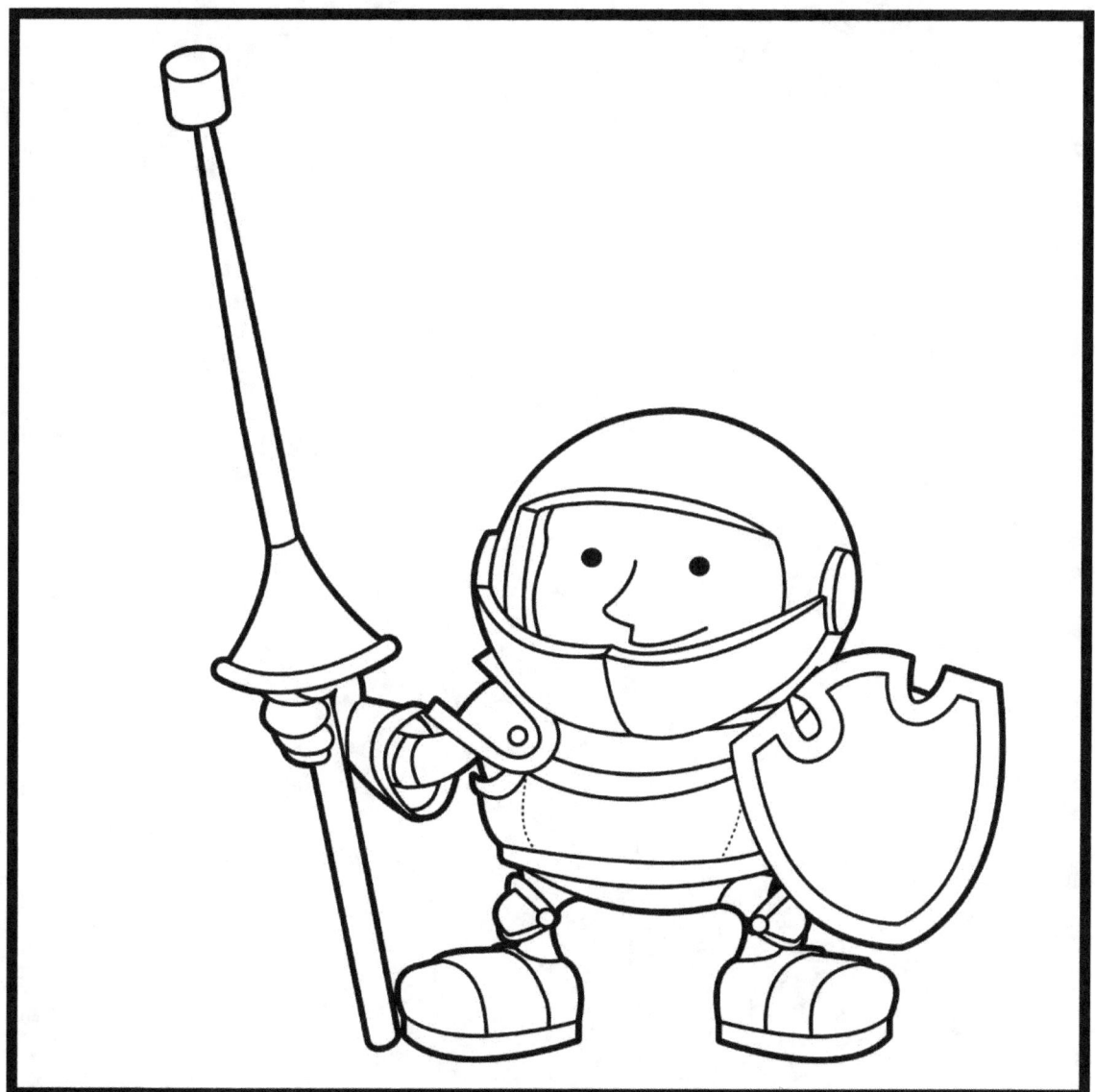

note:

_____

_____

_____

JULY 25TH

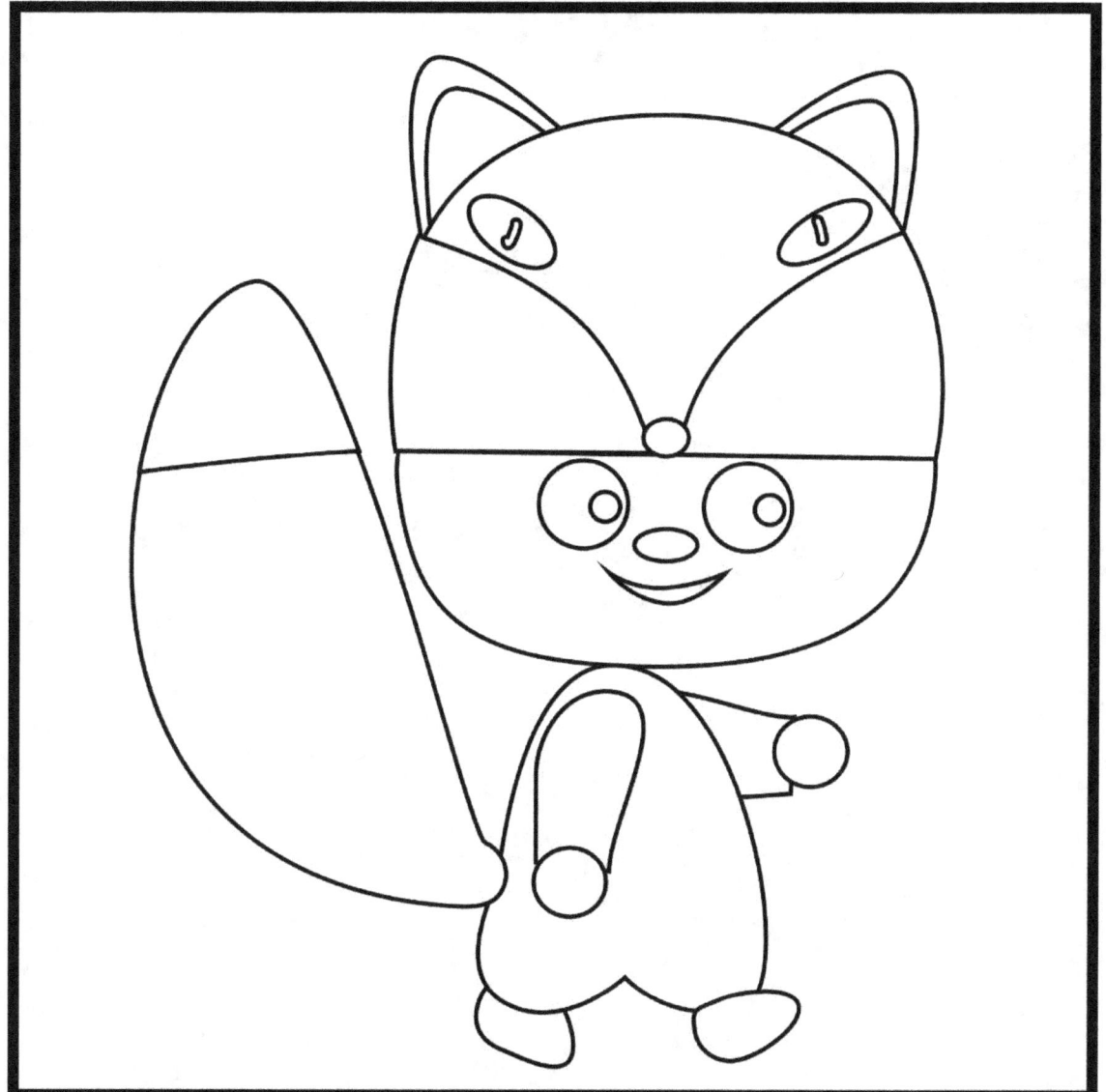

note:

_____

_____

_____

JULY 26TH

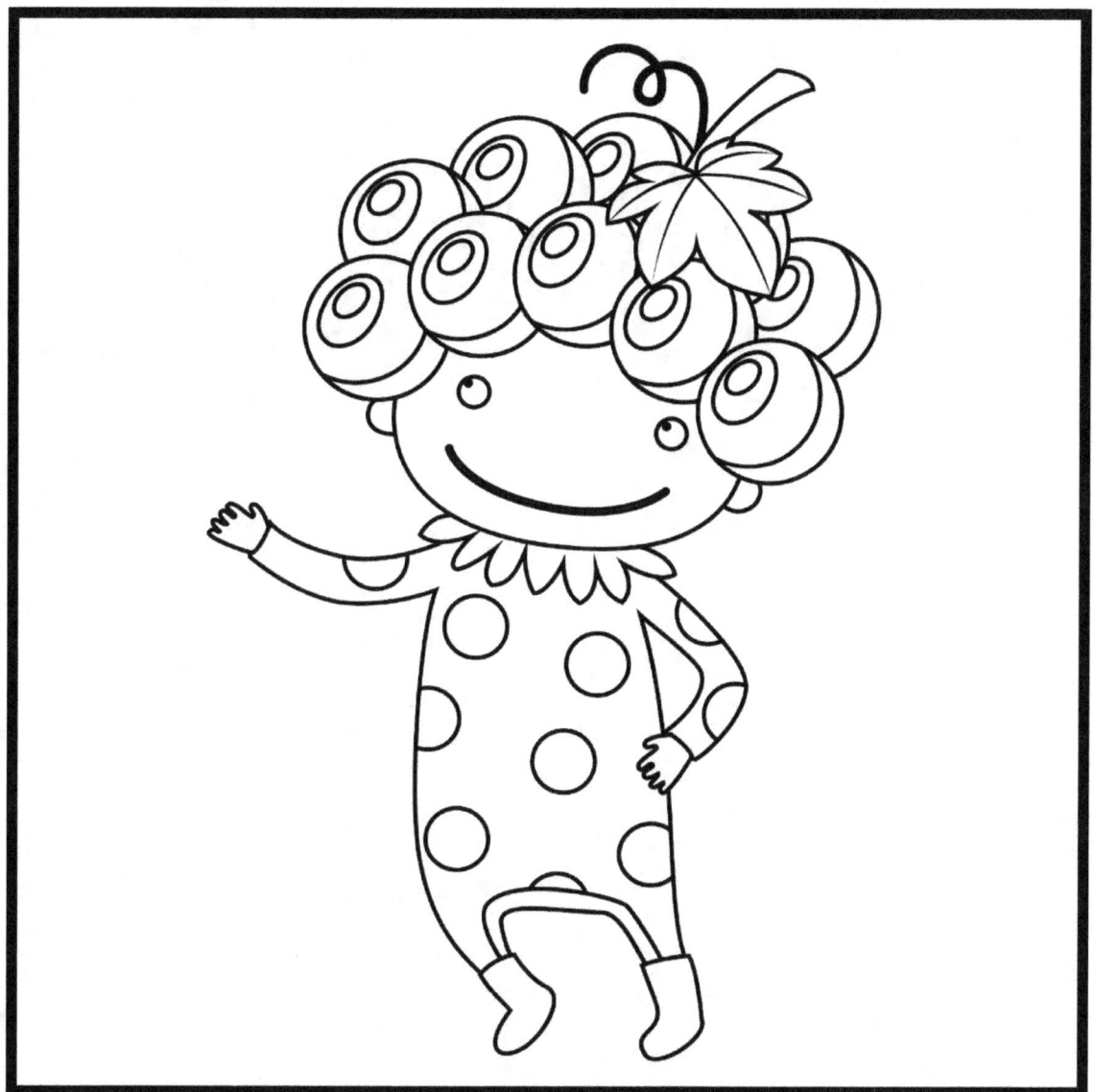

note:

_____

_____

_____

JULY 27TH

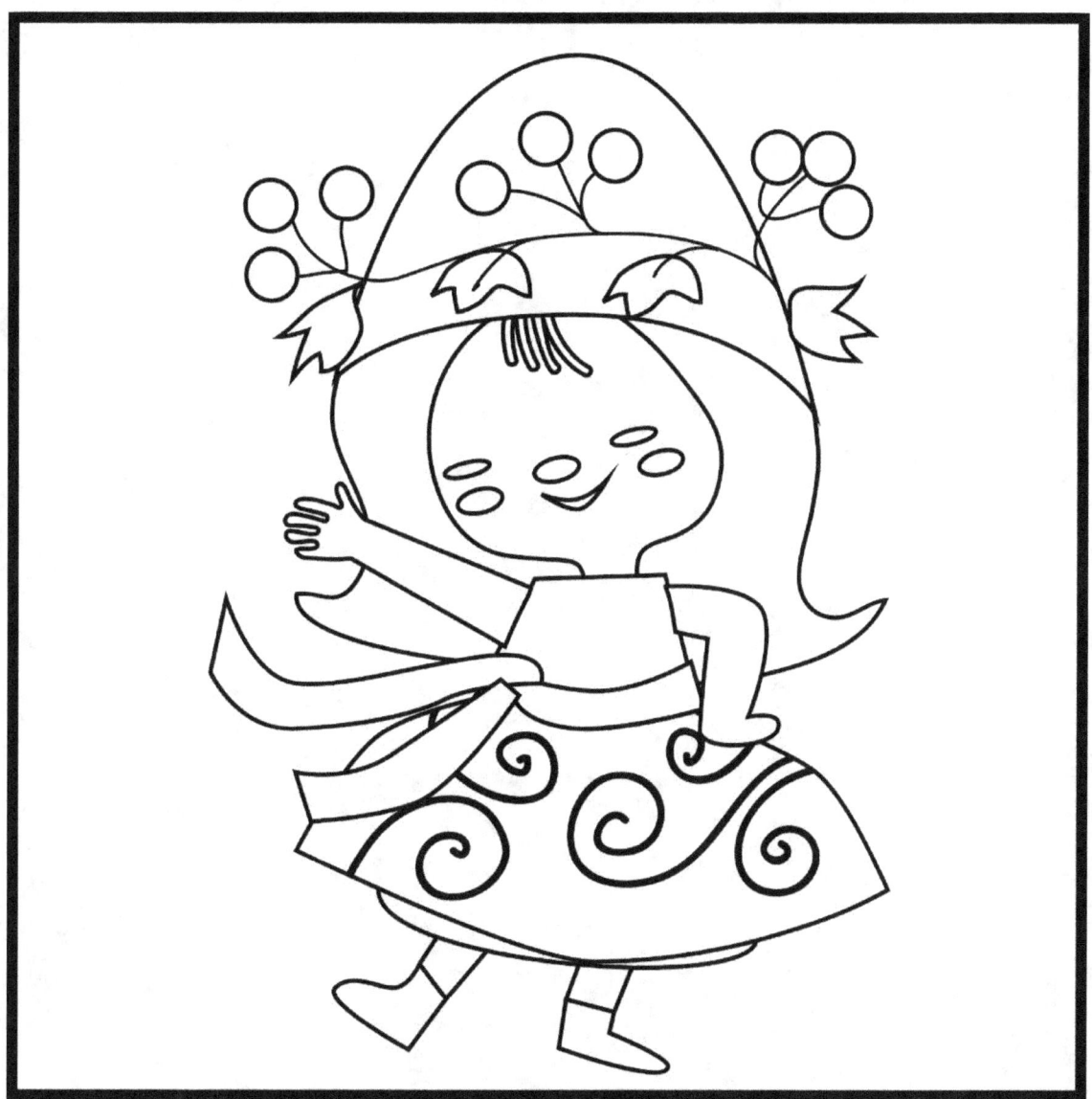

note:

_____

_____

_____

JULY 28TH

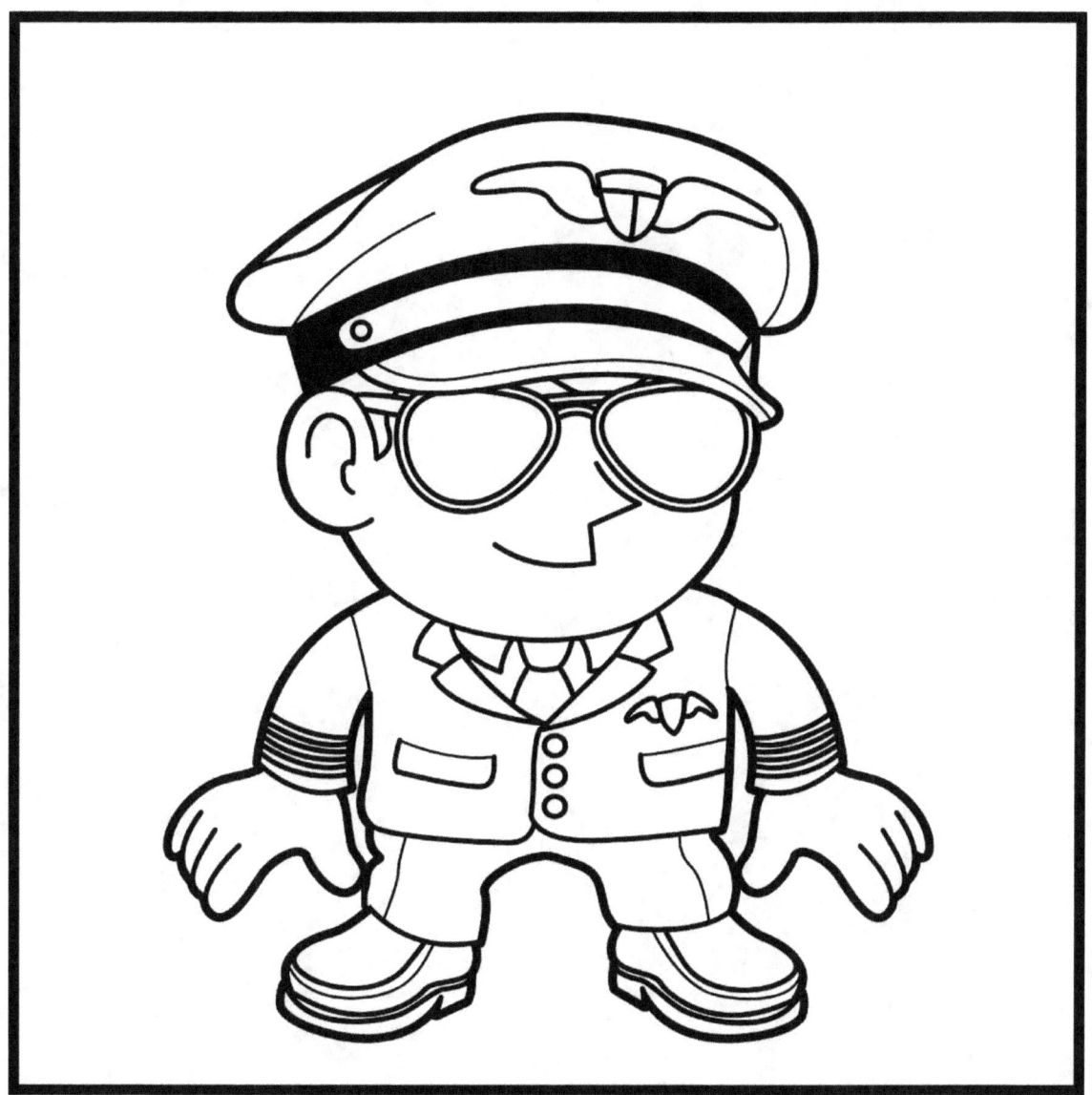

note:

_____

_____

_____

JULY 29TH

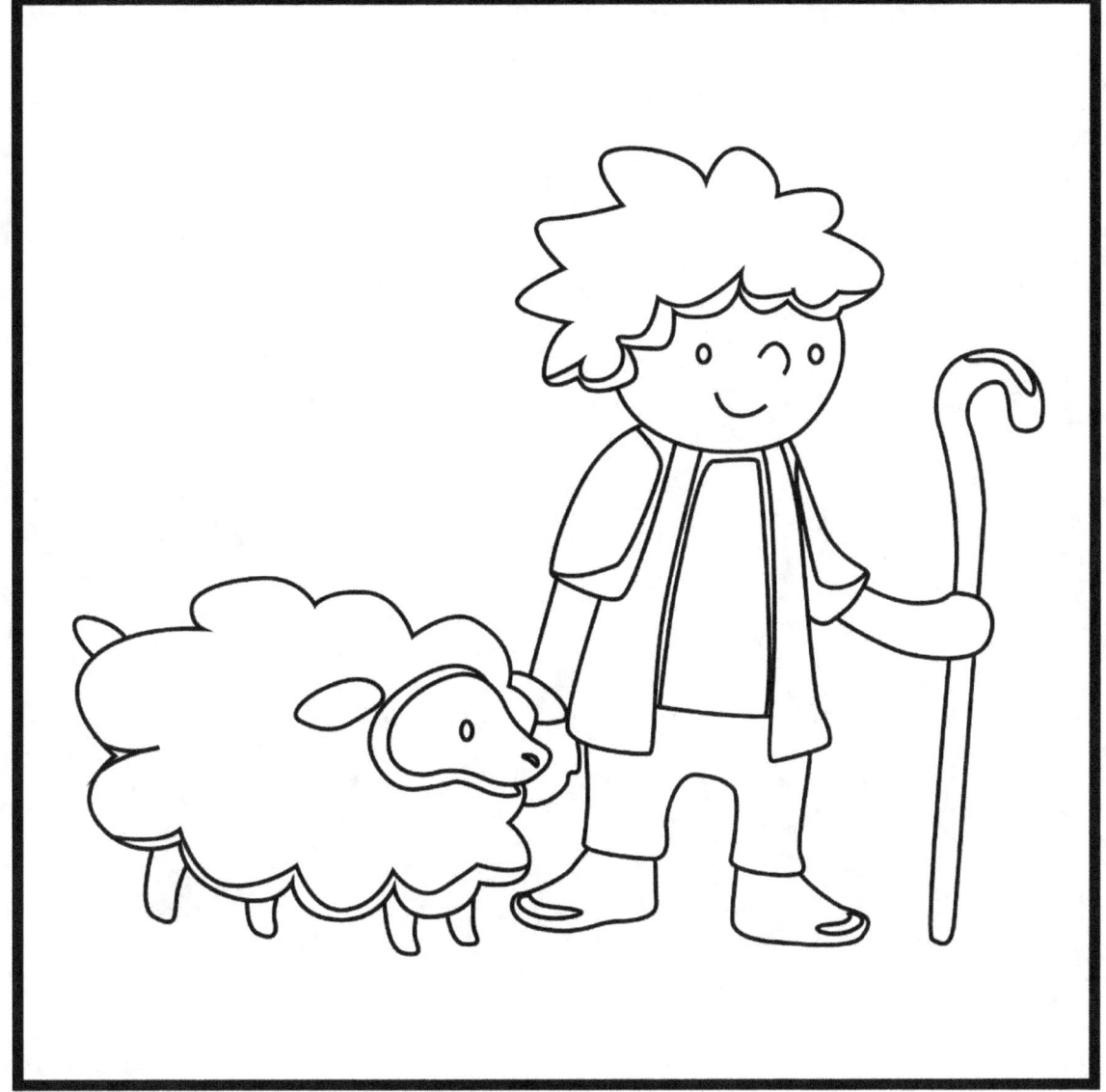

note:

_____

_____

_____

JULY 30TH

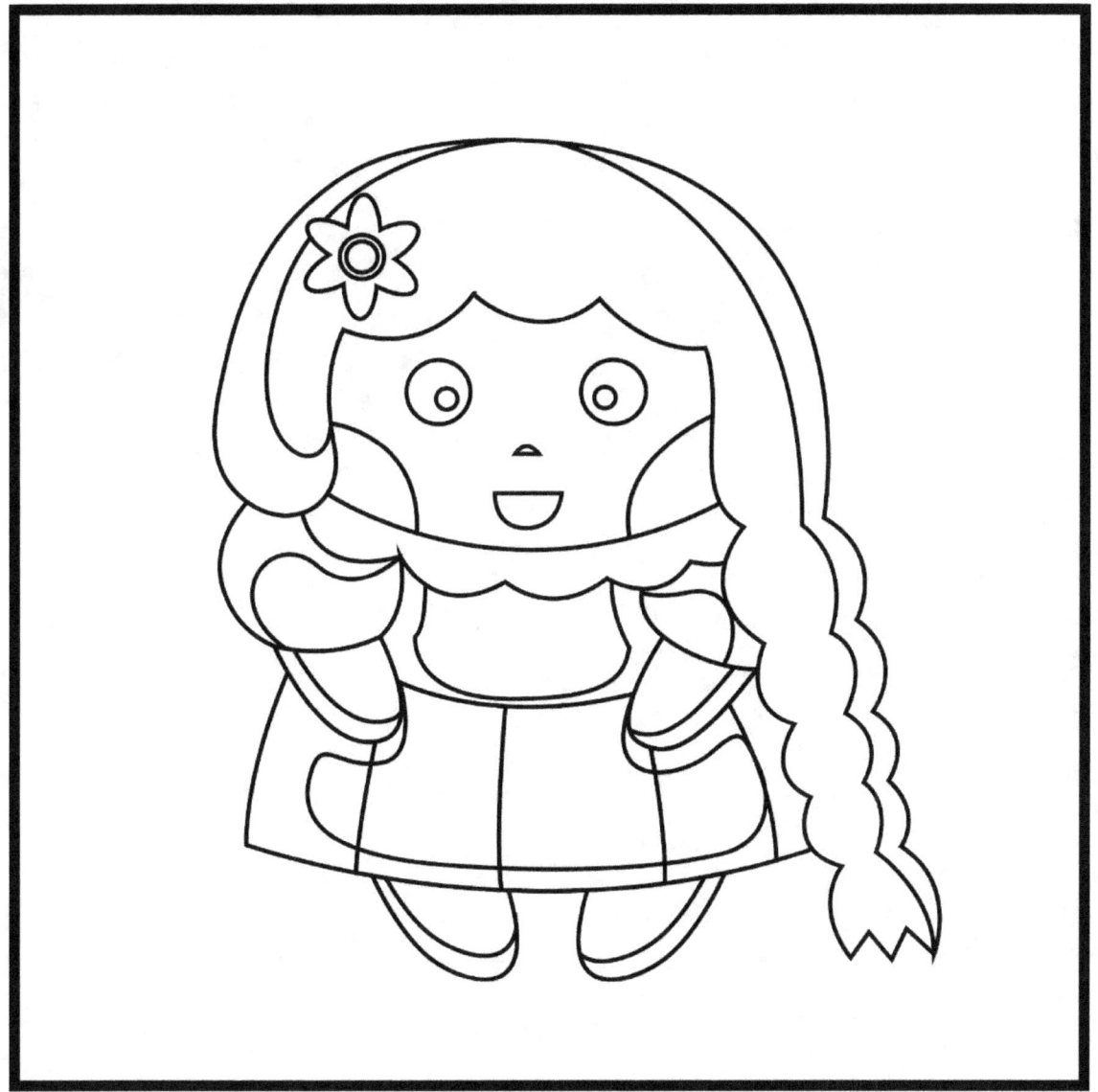

note:

_____

_____

_____

JULY 31TH

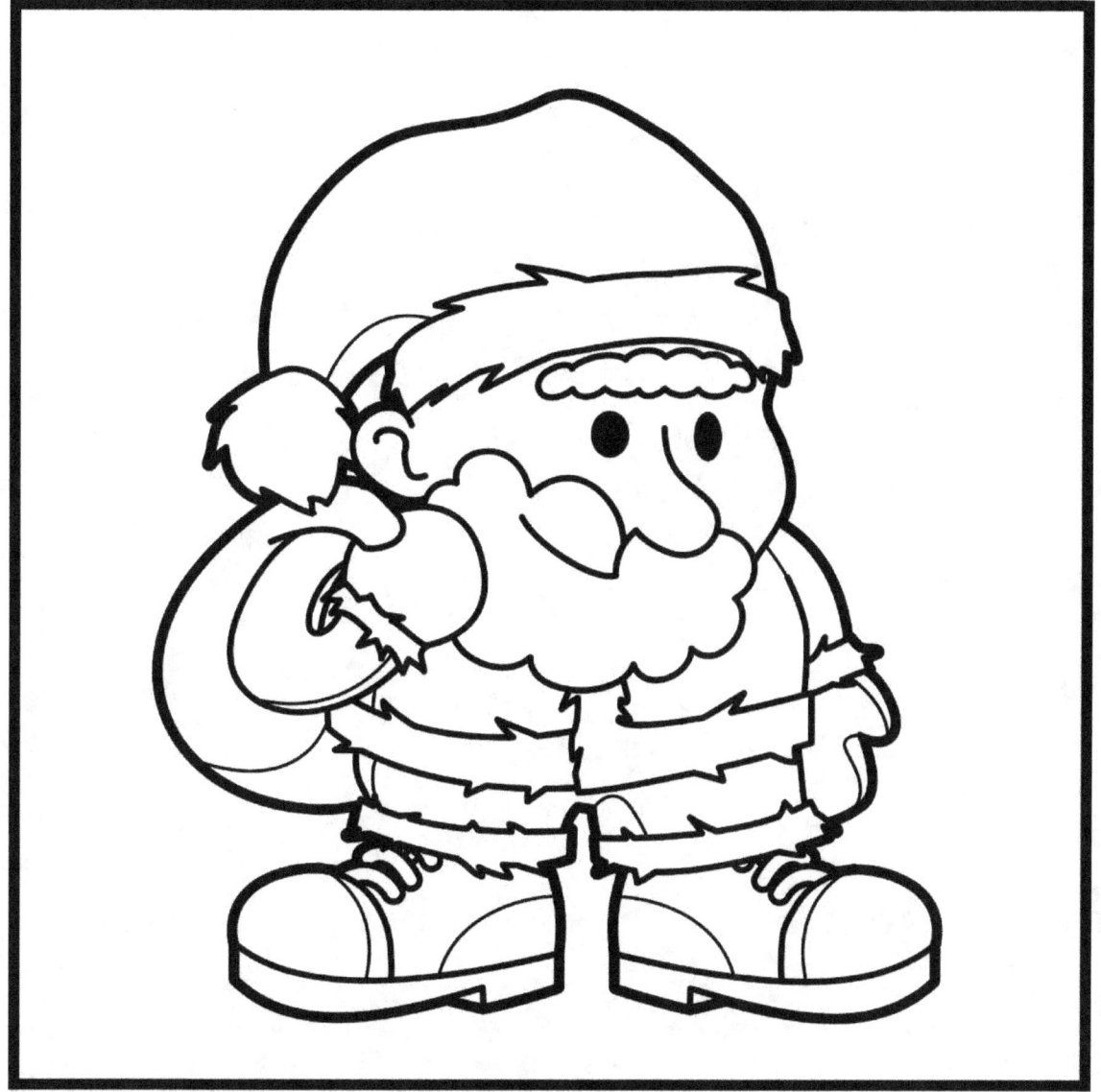

note:

_____

_____

_____

JULY 32TH

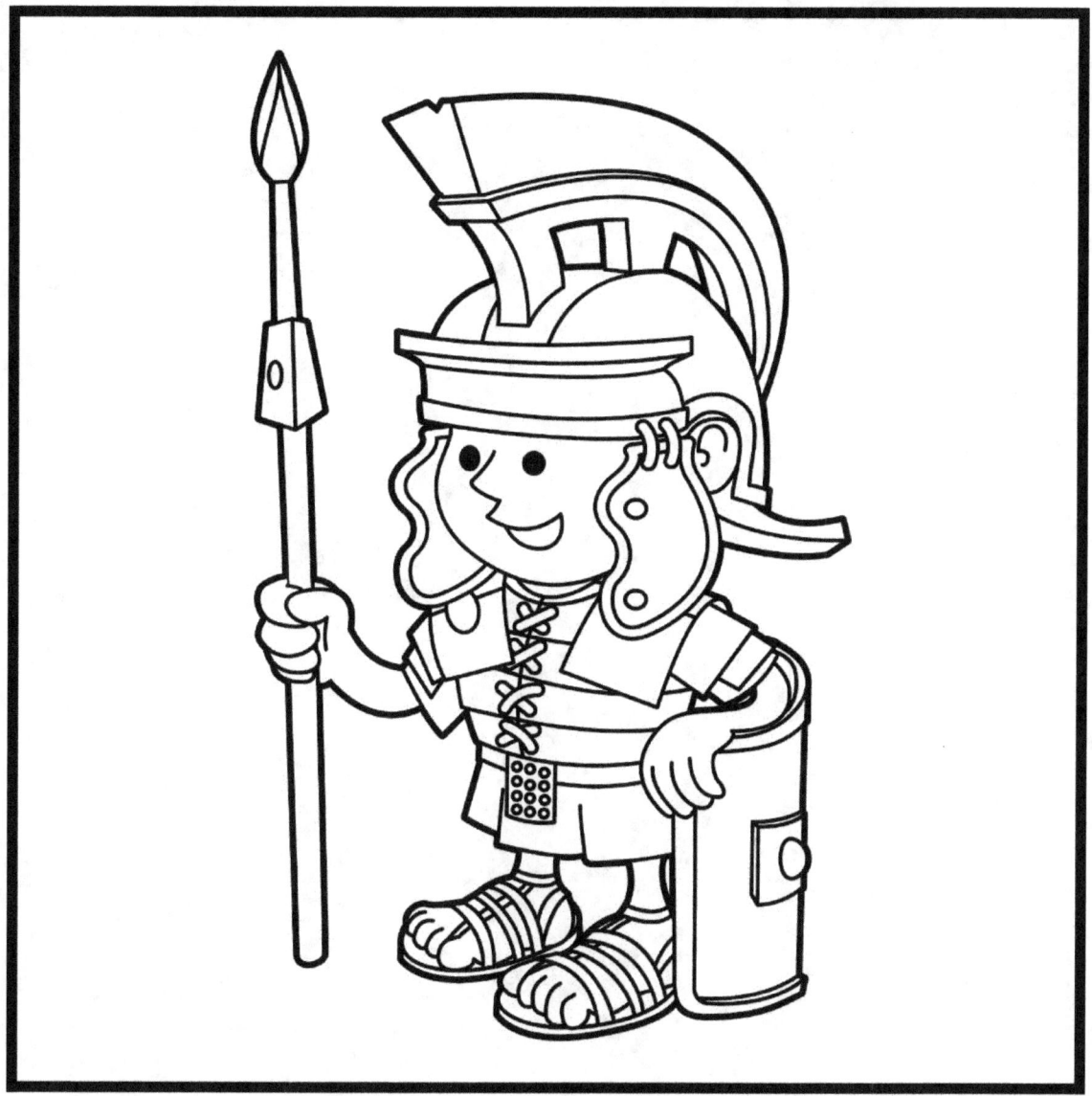

note:

_____

_____

_____

JULY 33TH

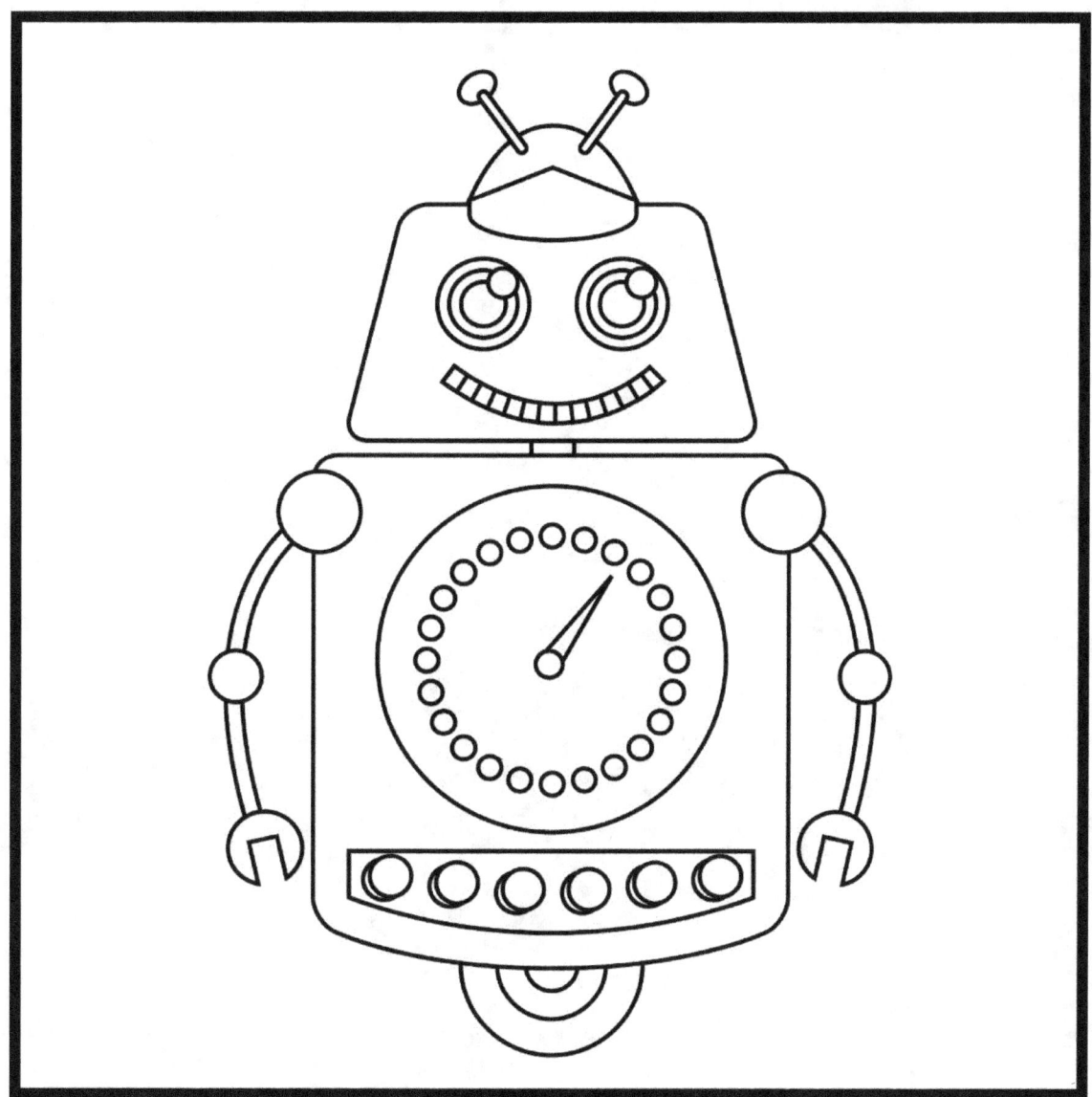

note:

_____

_____

_____

JULY 34TH

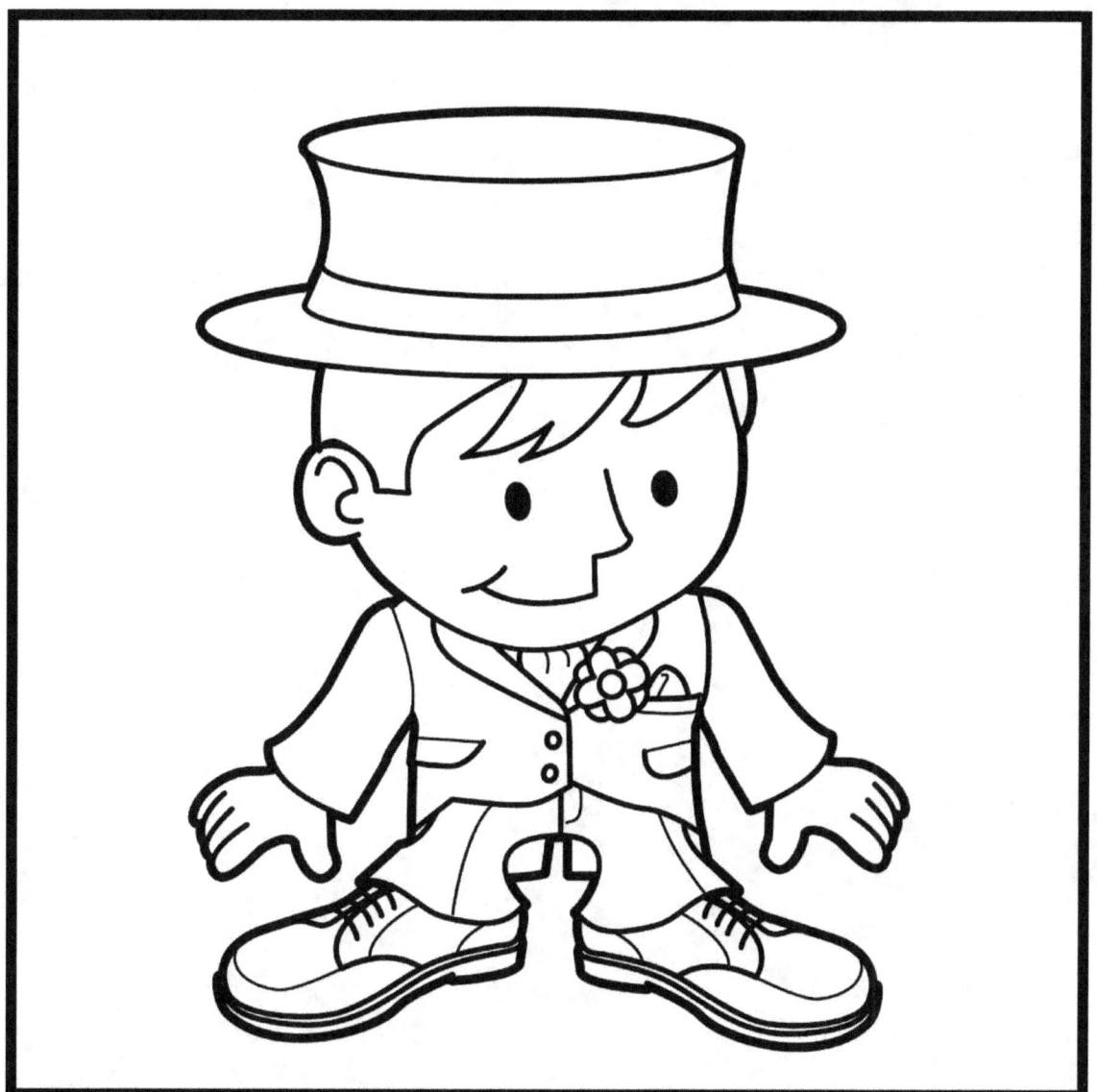

note:

_____

_____

_____

JULY 35TH

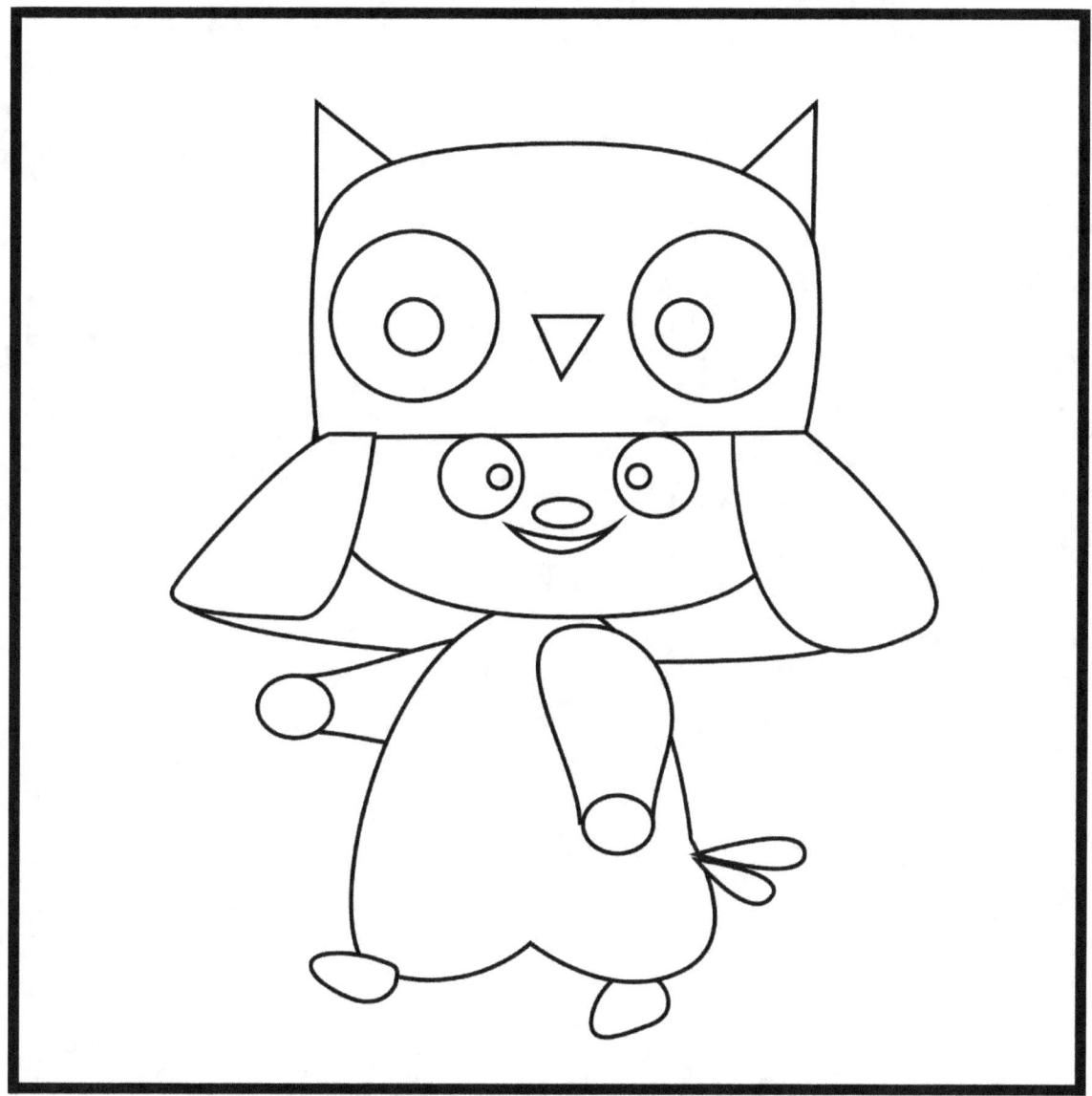

note:

_____

_____

_____

JULY 36TH

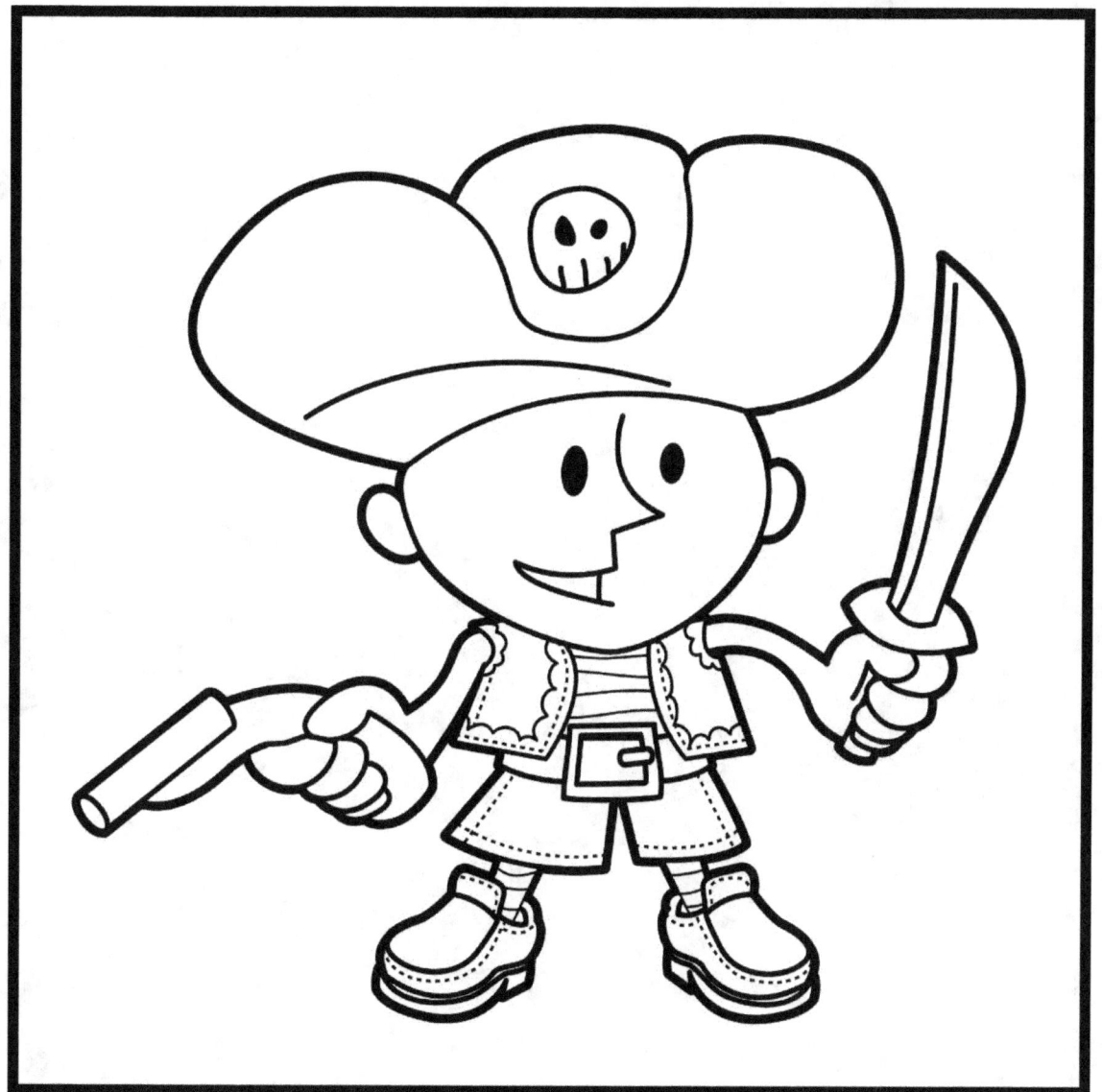

note:

_____

_____

_____

JULY 37TH

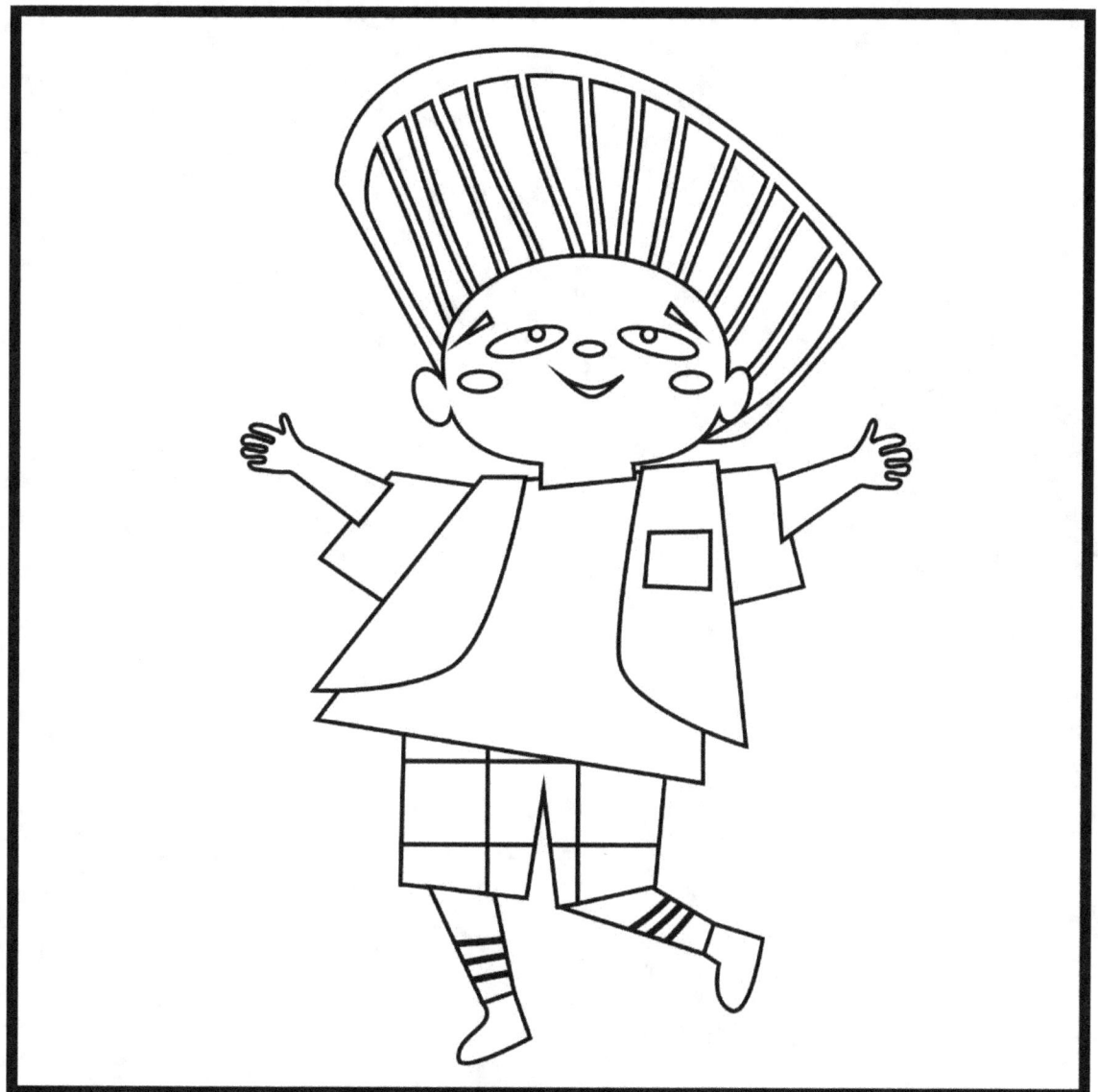

note:

_____

_____

_____

JULY 38TH

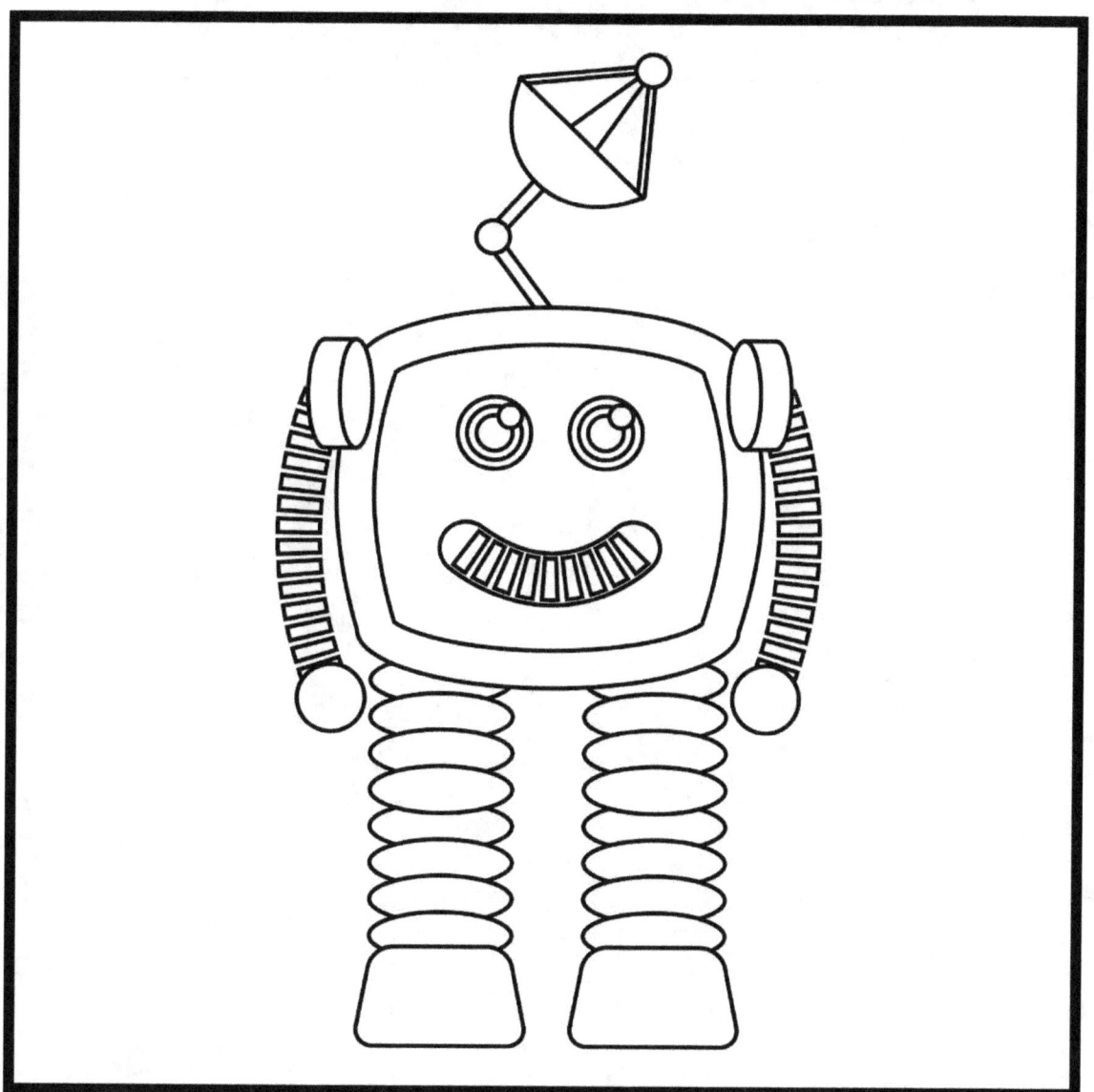

note:

_____

_____

_____

JULY 39TH

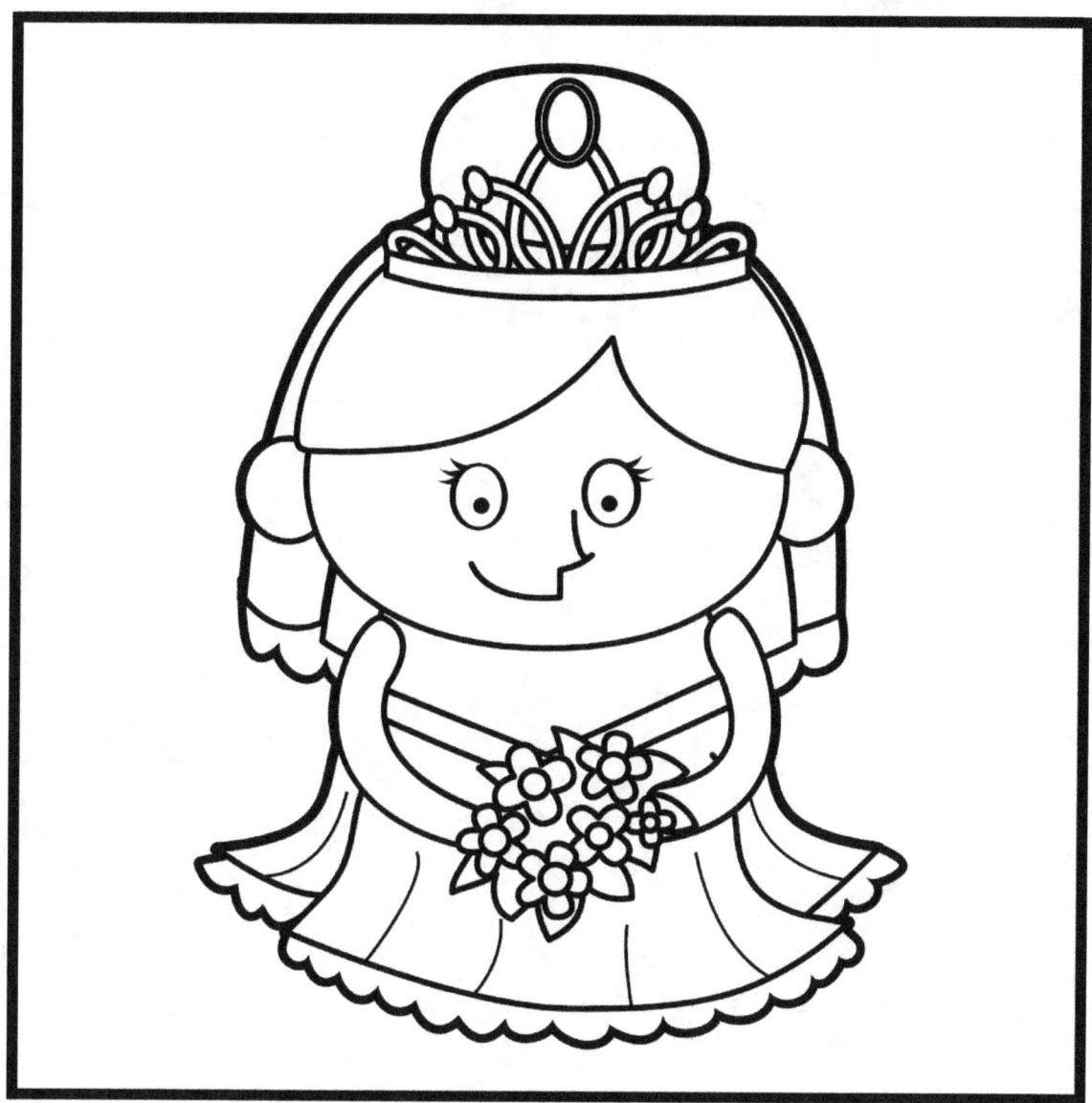

note:

_____

_____

_____

JULY 40TH

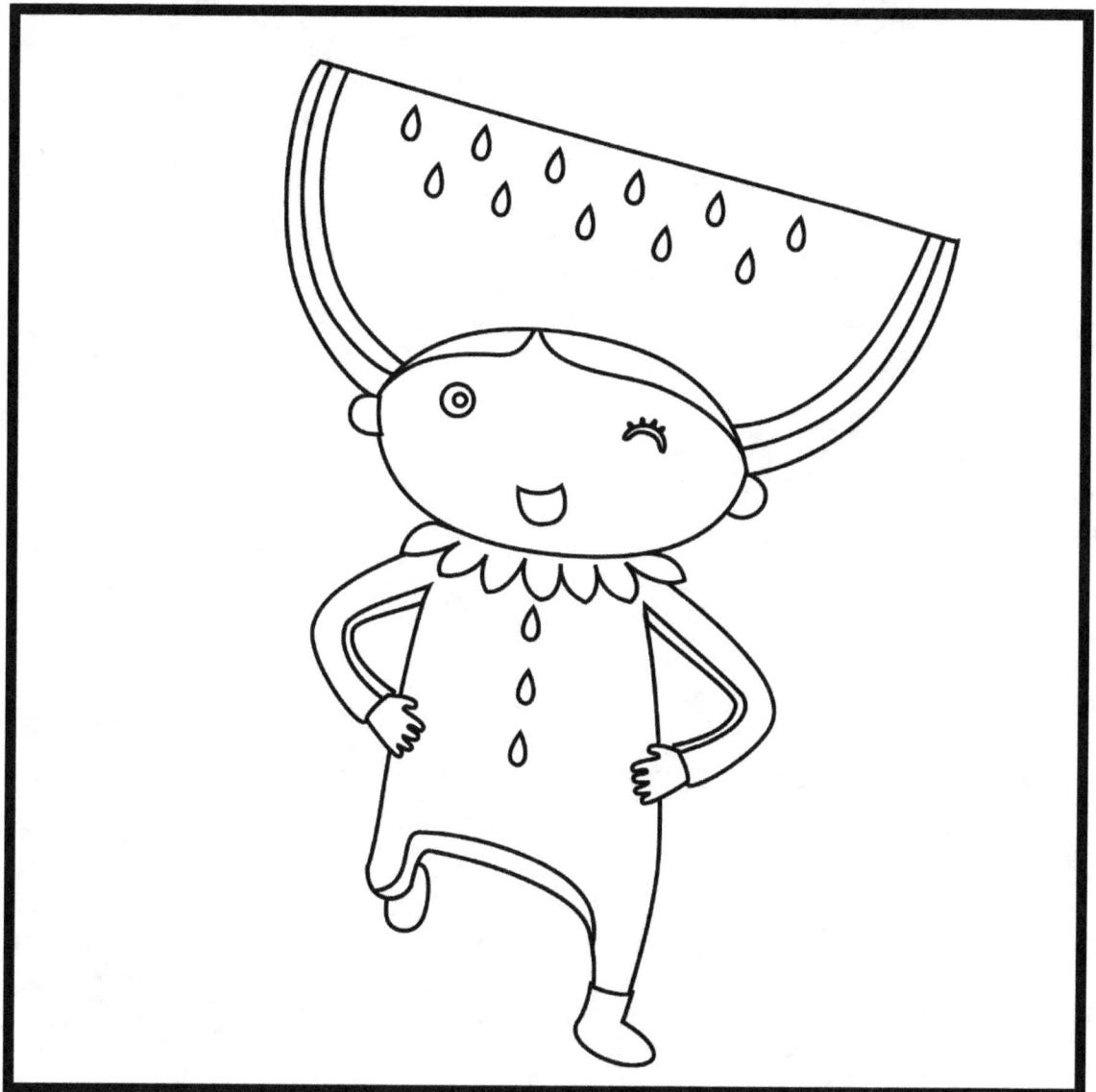

note:

_____

_____

_____

JULY 4TH

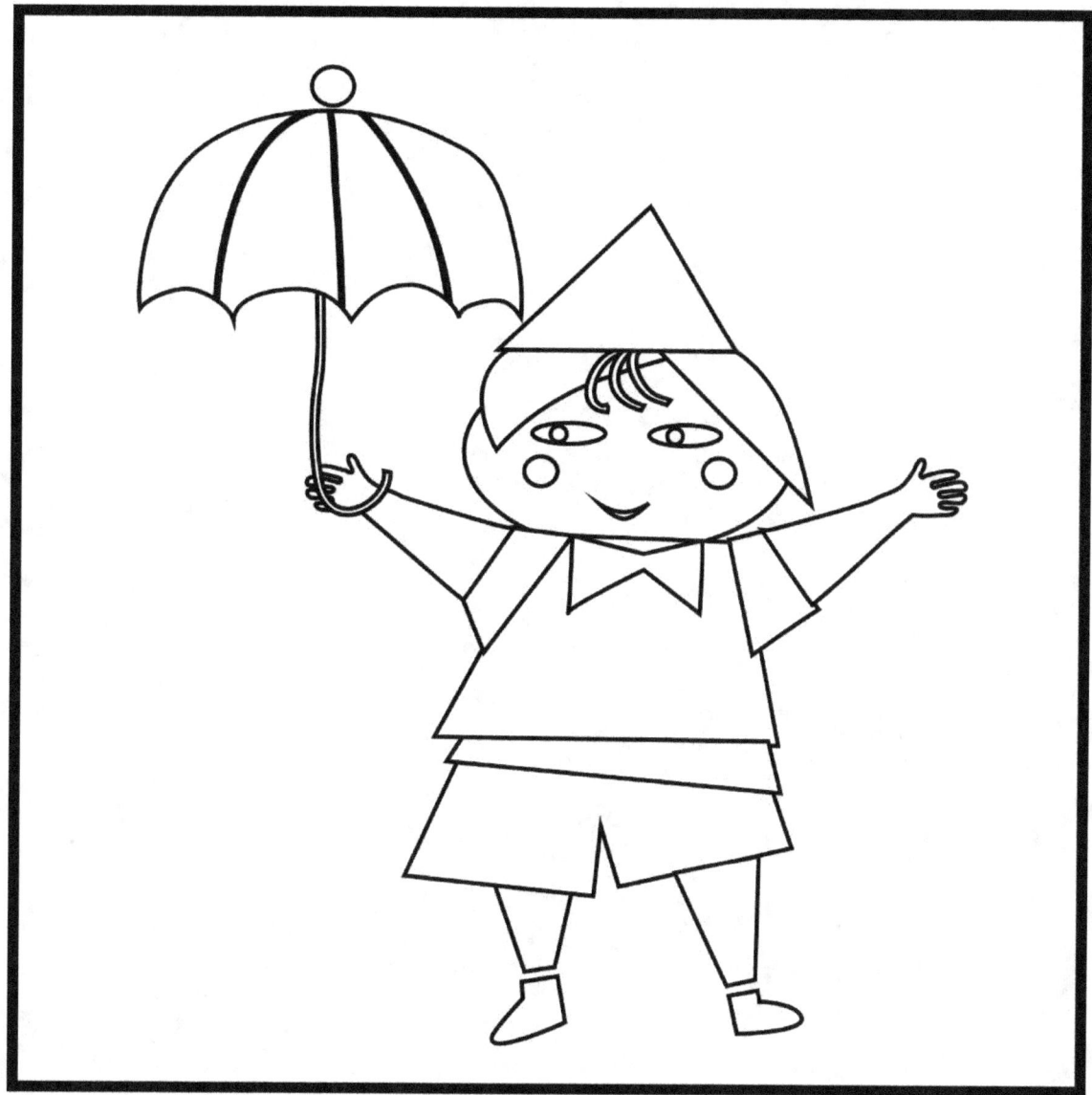

note:

_____

_____

_____

JULY 42TH

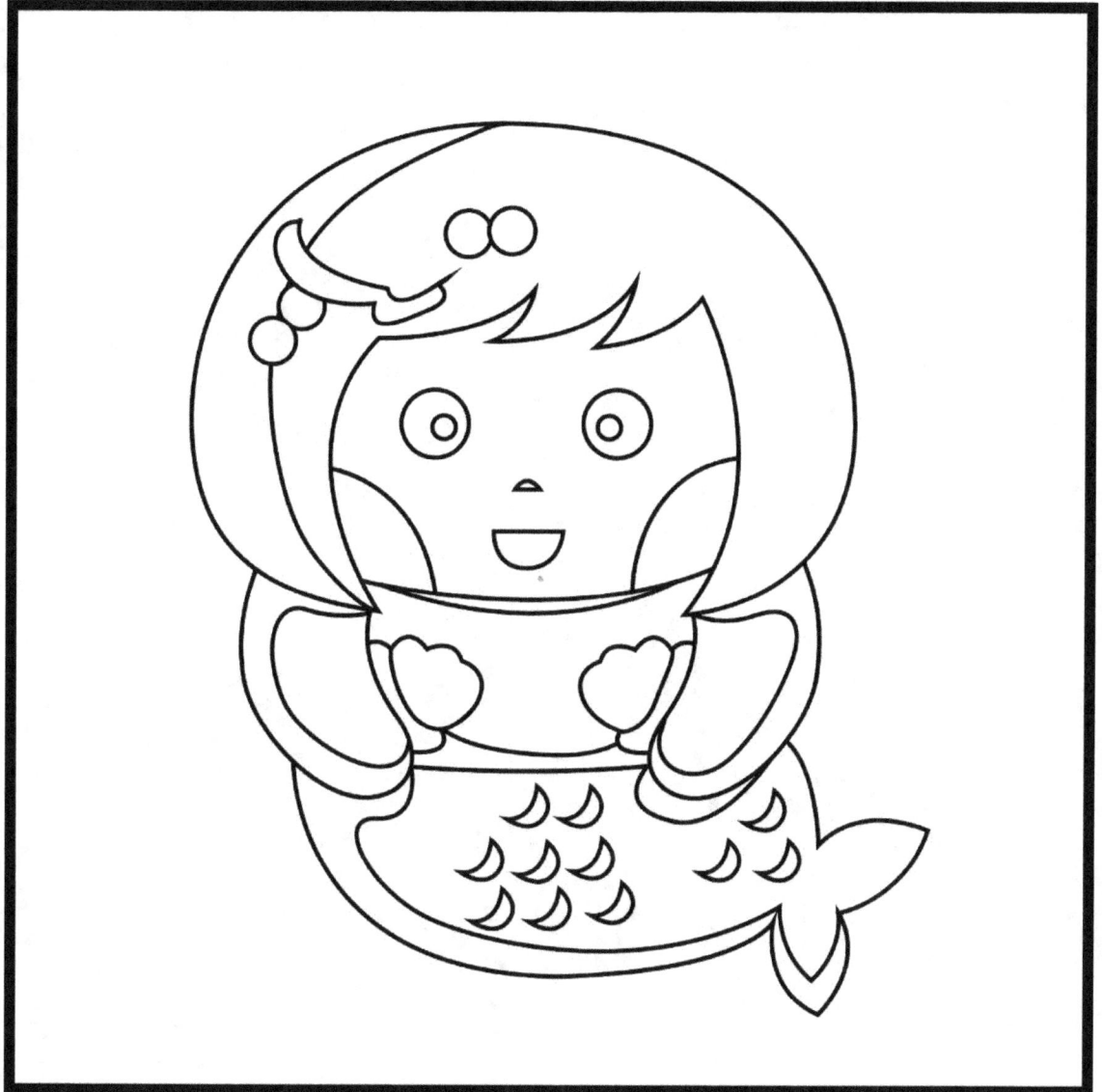

note:

_____

_____

_____

JULY 43TH

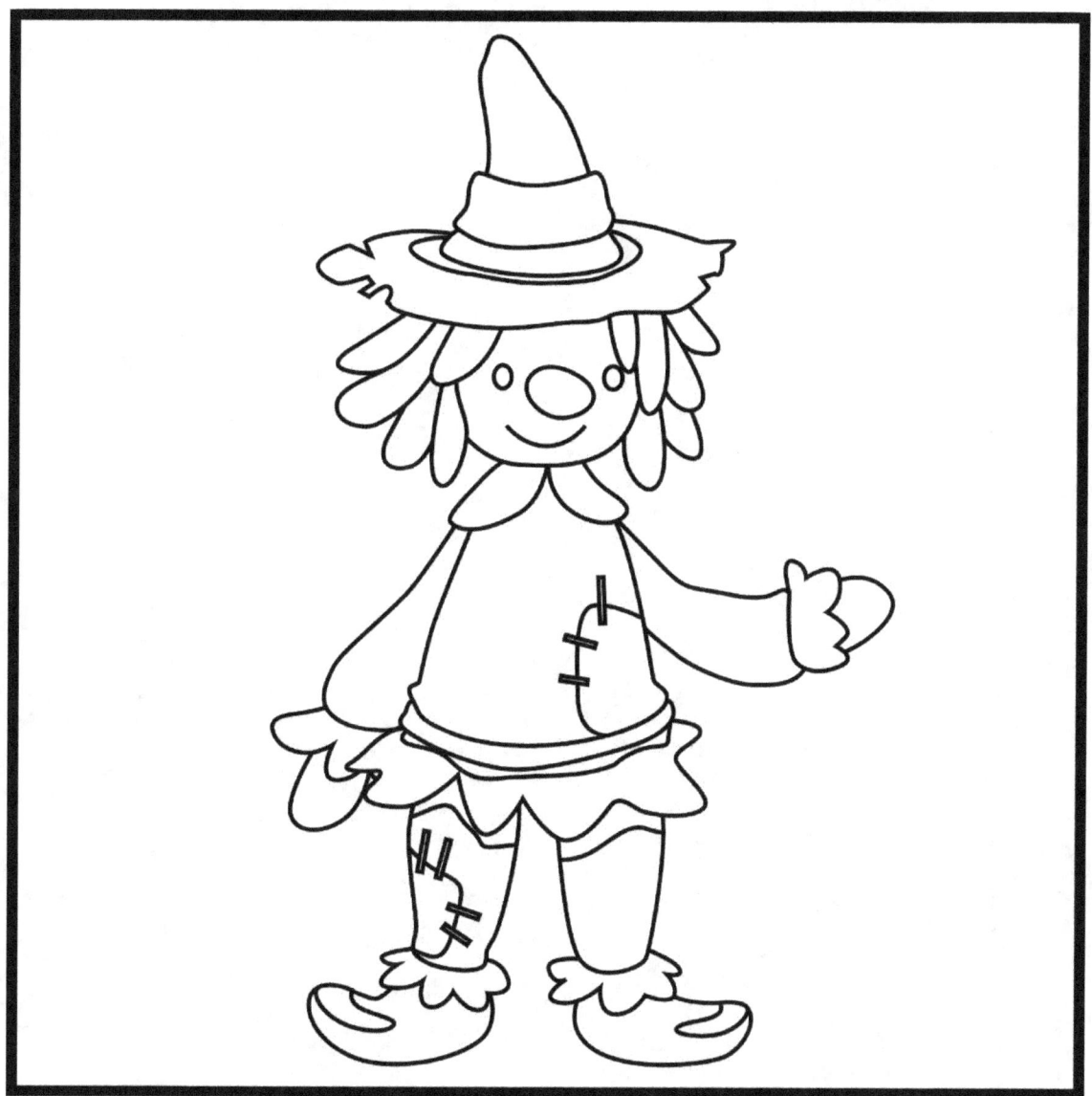

note:

_____

_____

_____

JULY 44TH

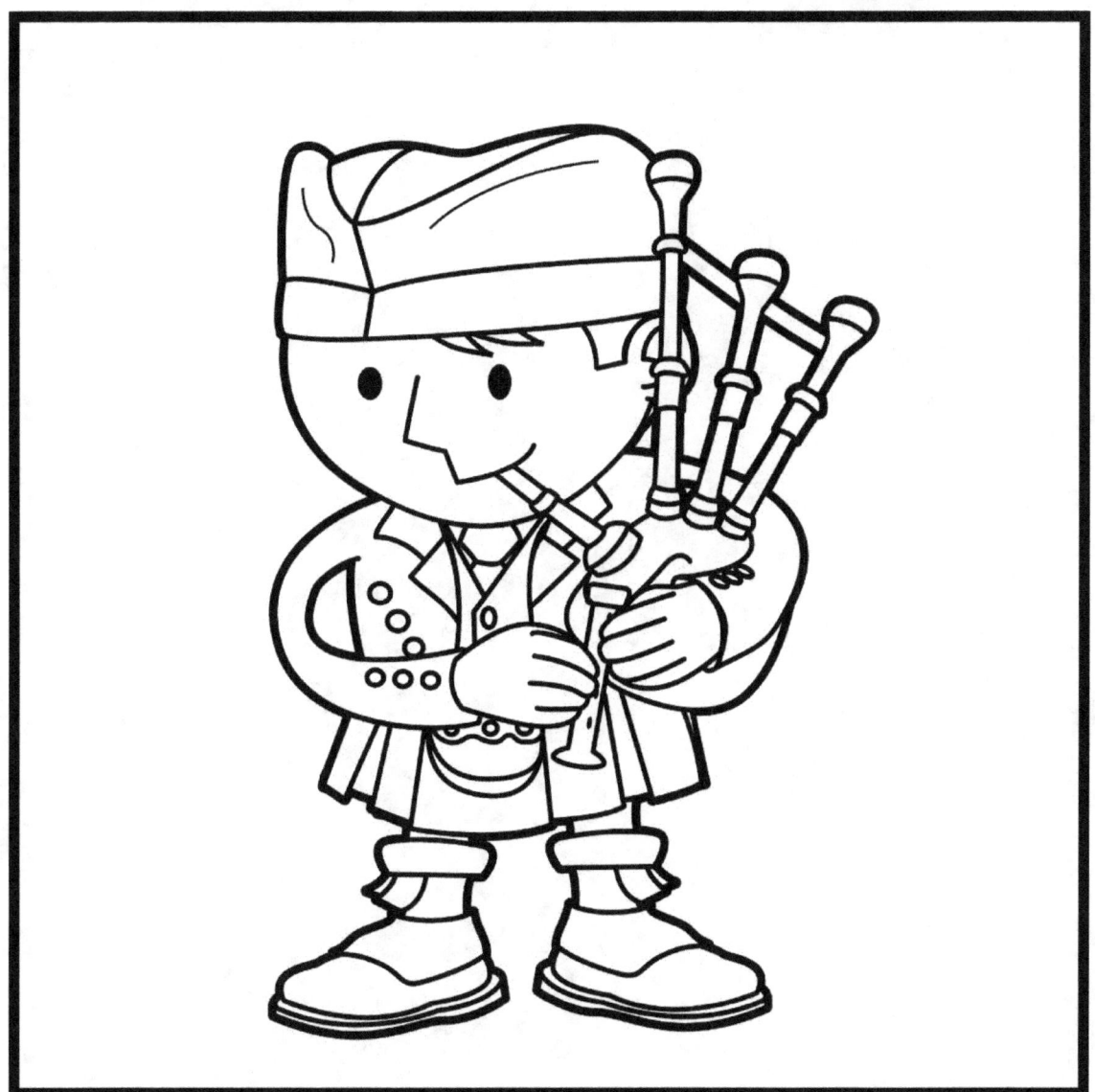

note:

_____

_____

_____

JULY 45TH

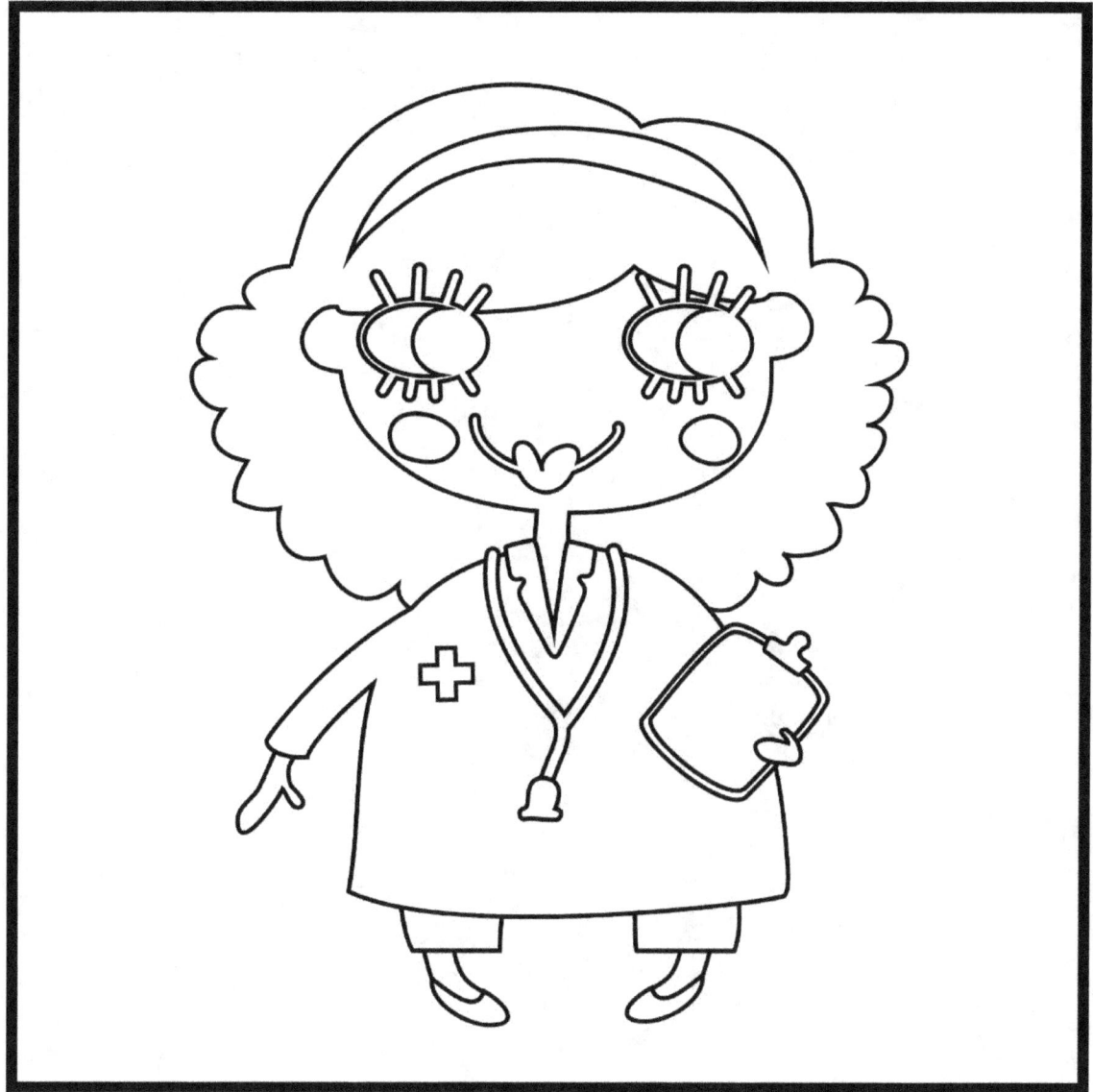

note:

_____

_____

_____

JULY 46TH

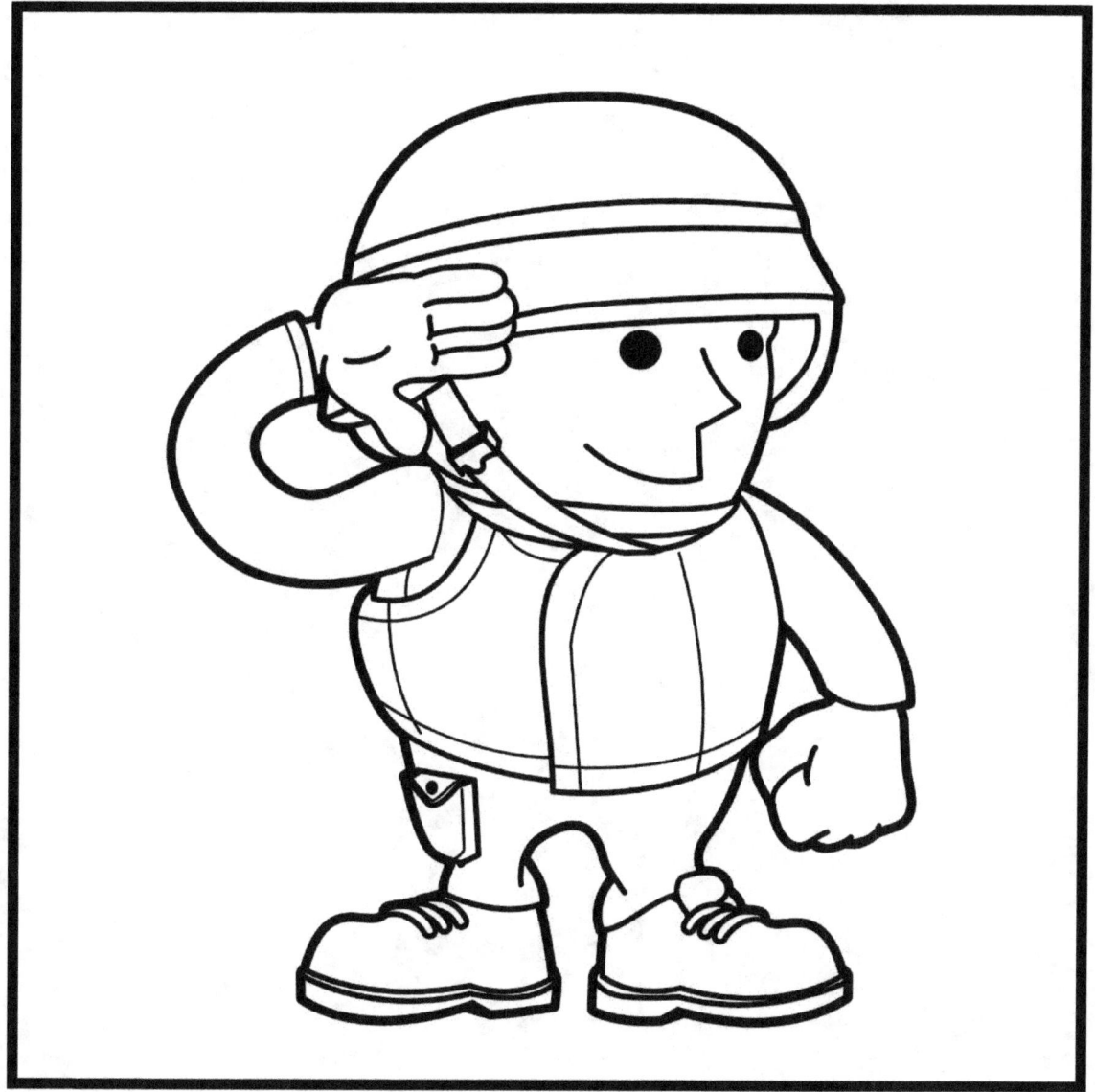

note:

_____

_____

_____

JULY 47TH

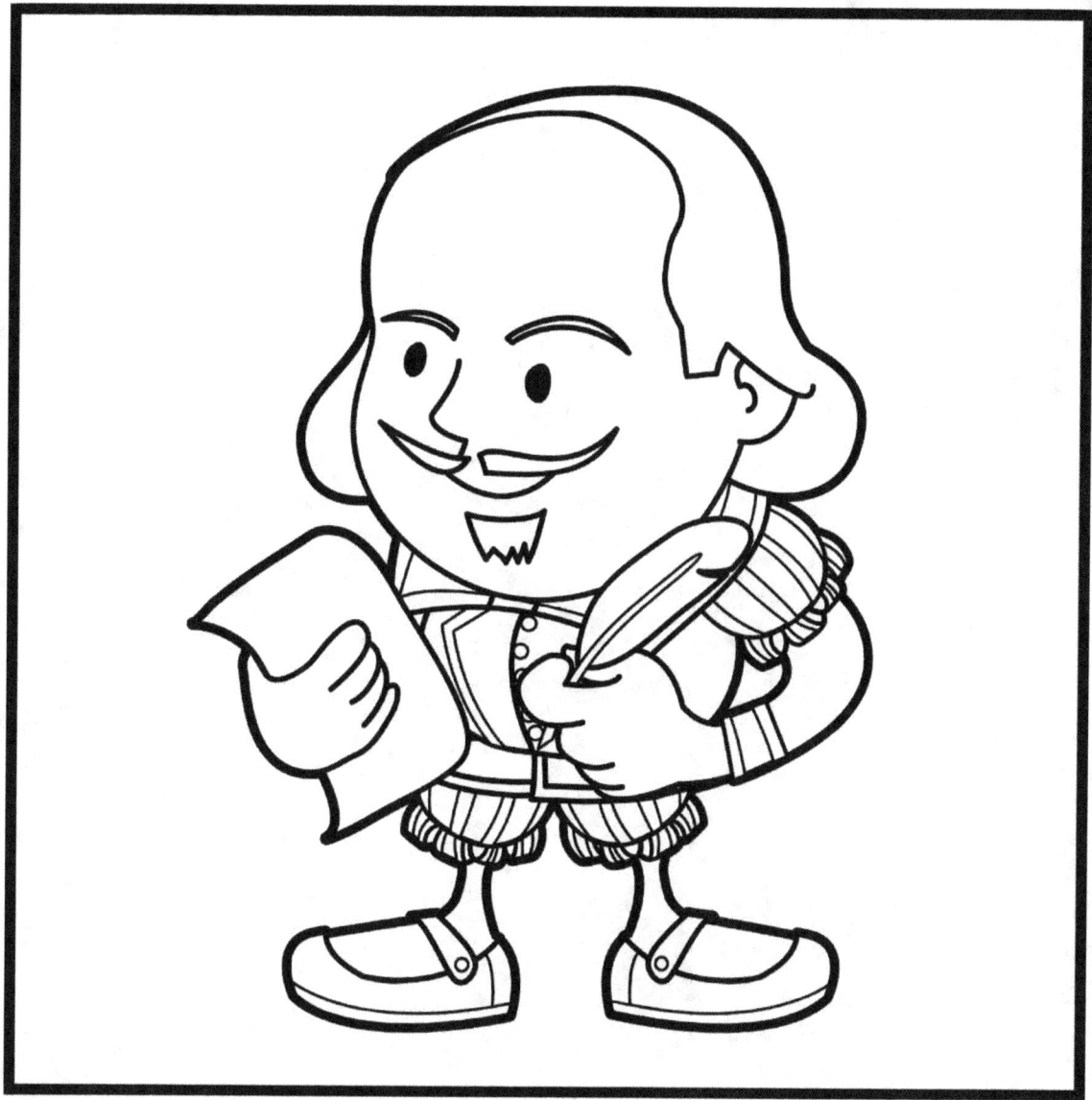

note:

_____

_____

_____

JULY 48TH

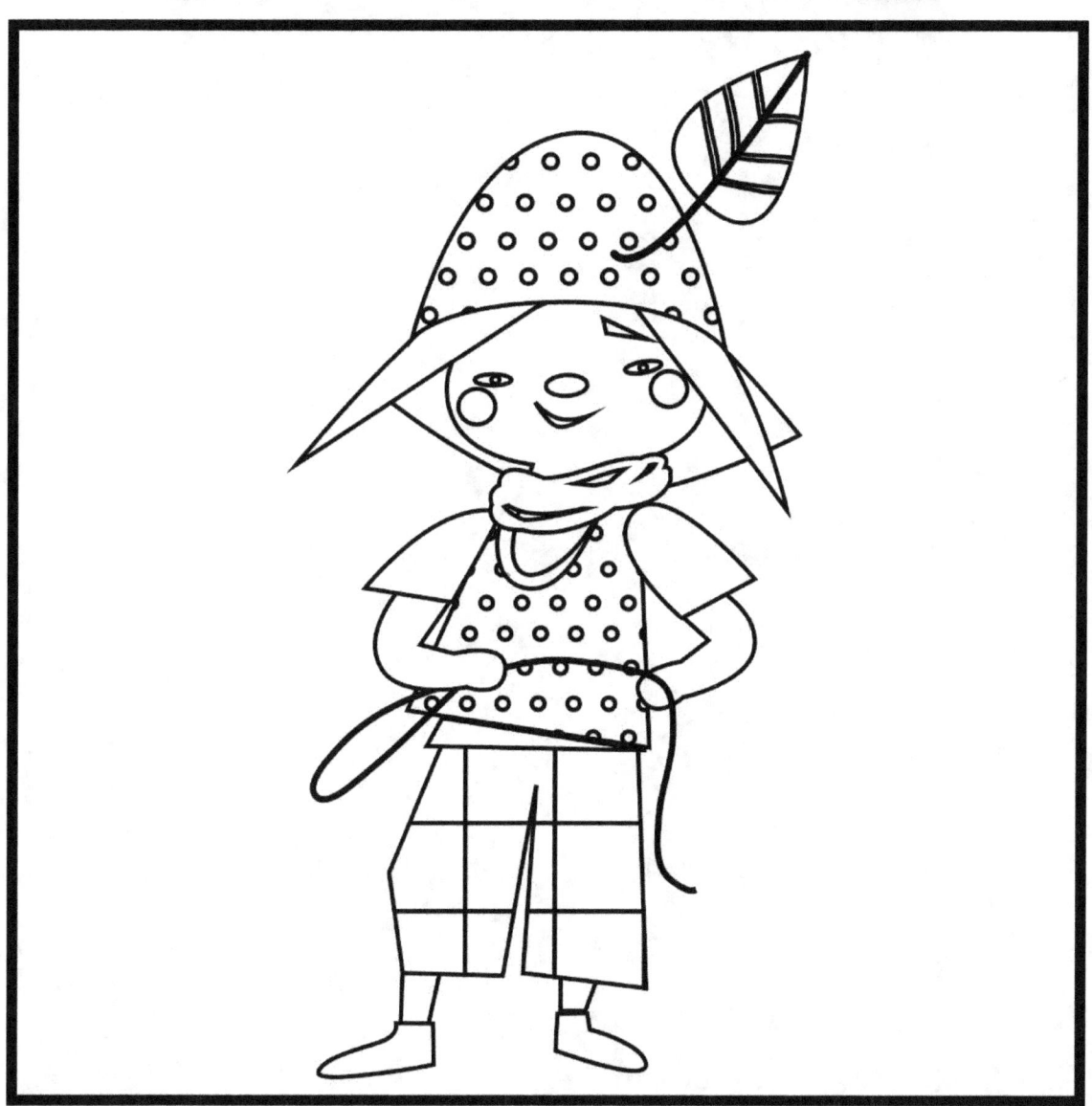

note:

_____

_____

_____

JULY 49TH

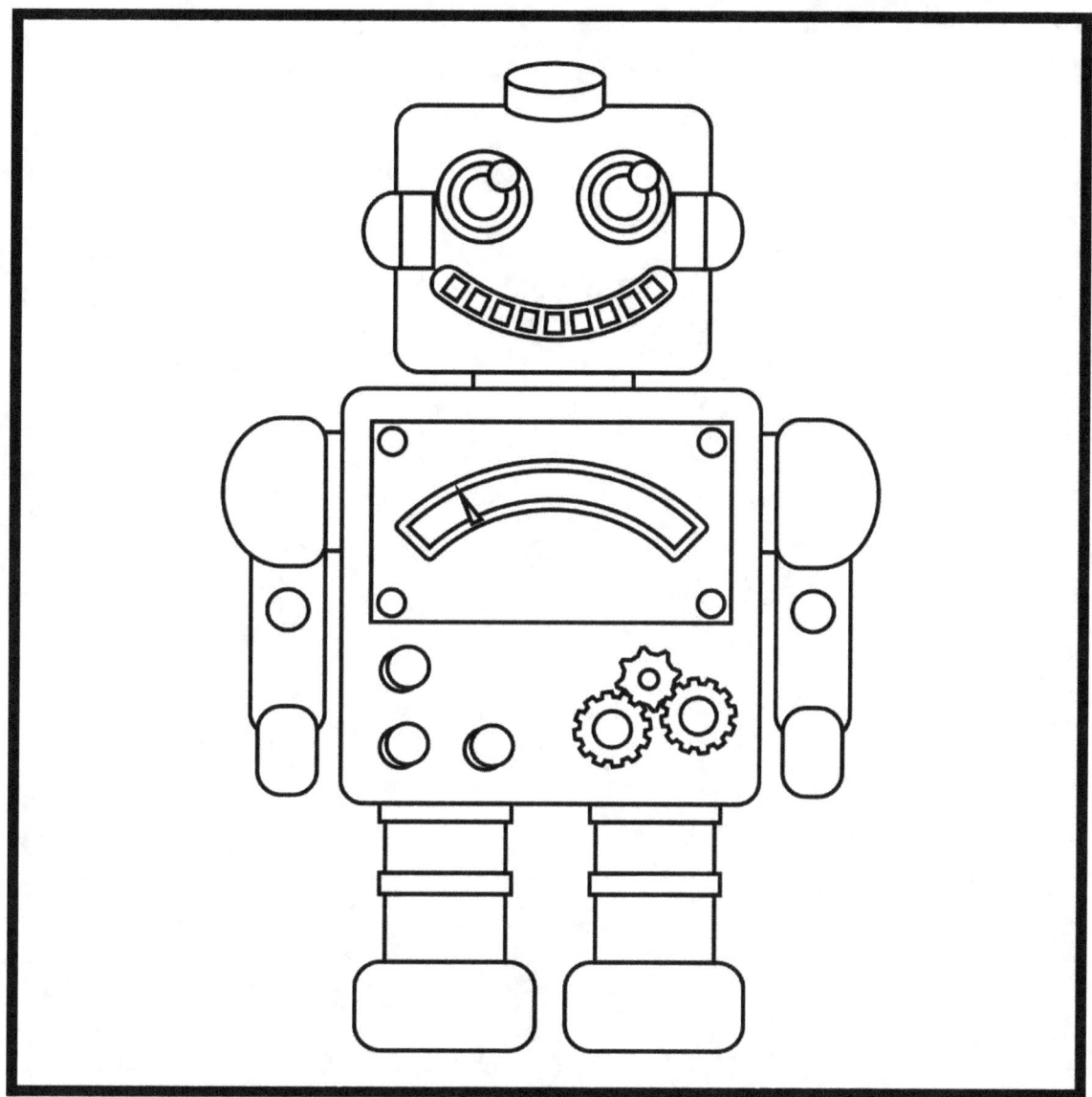

note:

_____

_____

_____

JULY 50TH

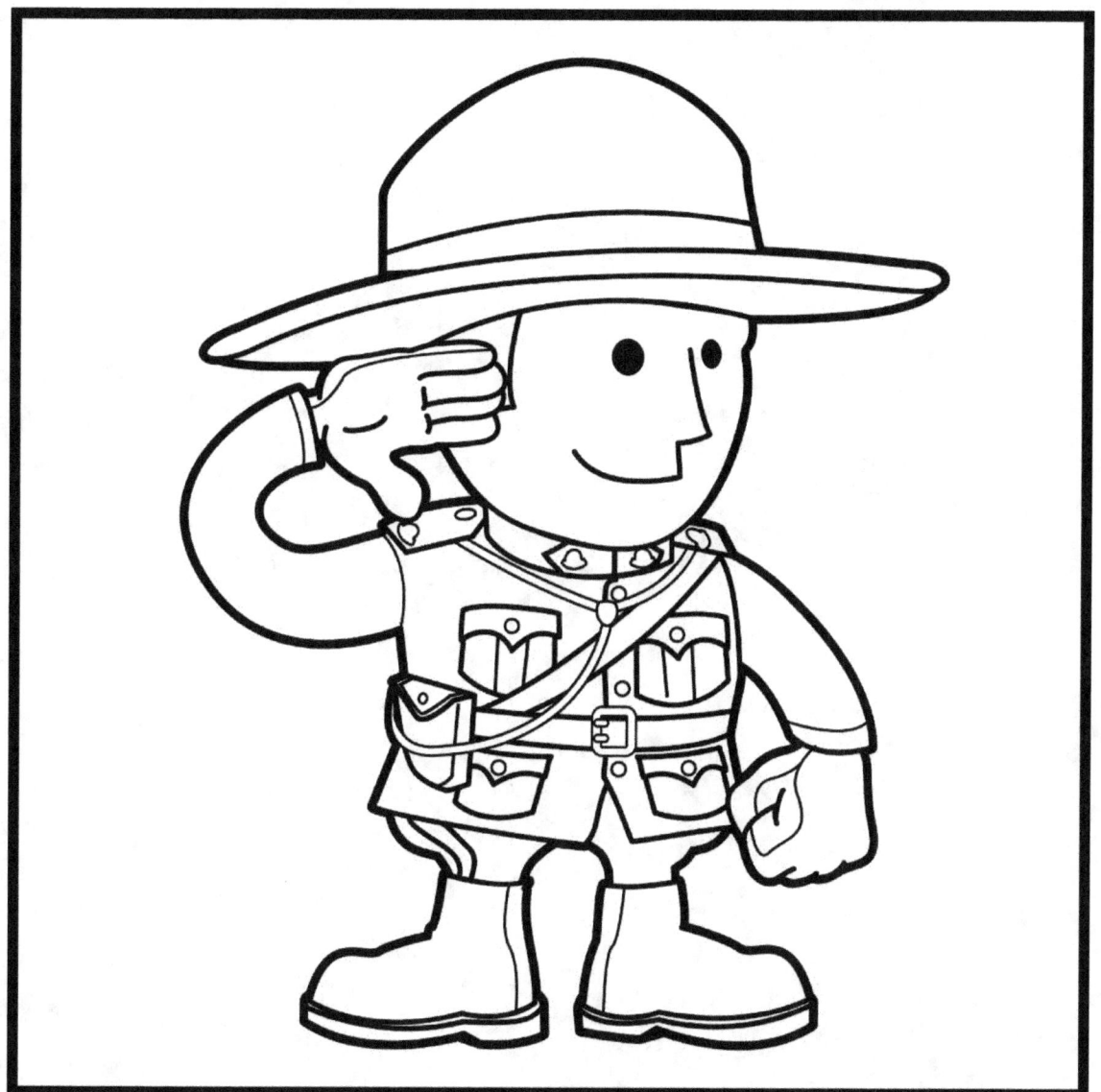

note:

_____

_____

_____